What people are saying about …

The Christian Athlete

"Brian is contributing much needed biblical understanding to one of the most powerful, culture-shaping mediums in the world—sports and competition. For the athletes and coaches who allow this content to help them integrate faith and sport, their athletic experience will be greatly enhanced!"

Mark Householder, president
of Athletes in Action

"As an Olympic softball player who loves Jesus, I wish I'd had this book in my hands when I was competing. Its timely message about combining faith and sport is needed more than ever for the days we are living in. It will impact Christian athletes in ways that will transcend the playing field for the rest of their lives."

Leah Amico, three-time Olympic Gold Medalist,
author of *Softball, Glory & God's Story*

"This is the best book I have read in the realm of sports and faith. Brian does a masterful job of drawing us closer to our King in the context of our athletic endeavors. Our culture is in desperate need of a book like this, as we as believers so often fail to integrate our faith into sports. This should be a required read for any Christian athlete, coach, or administrator who is seeking to glorify God through sports."

Dr. Tim Sceggel, director of athletics
and professor at Covenant College

"*The Christian Athlete* by Brian Smith is full of nuggets, wisdom, and everything you need to know about how to live out your faith as a Christian athlete. I believe this book will become the go-to read on this subject."

Jason Romano, director of media for Sports
Spectrum and author of *Live to Forgive*

"*The Christian Athlete* combines biblical instruction, theological insight, and practical wisdom to help athletes glorify God through the sports they play. Brian combines years of experience at the intersection of faith and sport in this unique and helpful book. It addresses and answers the question every Christian athlete should wrestle with: *What does God want from me as an athlete?*"

Chris Maragos, two-time Super Bowl
champion, host of the *Mission of Truth* podcast

"For thirty-three seasons as the Detroit Lions chaplain (I know … lots of losses), I worked with hundreds of athletes who were all asking, 'How do I apply my faith on the field?' I wish I'd had this book. Brian lays out a comprehensive vision of how God wants to work in and through the athlete who is committed to Him. This is a vision we all need for life on and off the field."

Dave Wilson, cohost of *Family Life
Today,* former Detroit Lions chaplain

"Brian Smith marvelously intersects the worlds of athletics and Christianity. *The Christian Athlete* is a practical roadmap for both the novice and the seasoned athlete. As a leading voice in Christian athletics, Brian presses into relevant cultural topics that are difficult to discern and define. *The Christian Athlete* arms athletic directors, coaches, and athletes to engage with culture where they are at. Whether you are striving to grow in your faith or intent on being a person of influence, this book is a must-read."

Ross Douma, director of athletics
at Dordt University

"Brian Smith does a phenomenal job of using Scripture and practical advice to help not just athletes but coaches and administrators as well to glorify God through sports. This book is one that I definitely plan on reading with my two young sons when they grow up and start playing sports at a competitive level."

Lee De Leon, cofounder and
president of ADs for Christ

"One of the things I love about Brian's writing is that it comes from years of experience as an athlete and a minister to and with athletes. In this book, Brian draws on that experience to provide a thoughtful and practical guide to the questions, concerns, and issues that many Christian athletes wrestle with as they try to live out their faith in sports. *The Christian Athlete* is an excellent addition to the growing conversation on Christian engagement with sports, useful for both athletes and those who work with them."

Paul Putz, PhD, assistant director
of the Faith & Sports Institute

"How should a Christian athlete think about winning and losing? What about pressure and practice and platform? While reading *The Christian Athlete*, I was repeatedly reminded how frequently we as Christian athletes need to commit our lives to win, lose, tie, and compete in a distinctly Christian way. I've played tackle football for over two decades and still need to be taught and reminded what being a holy competitor actually looks like. From riding the bench to retirement, Brian has words of wisdom and encouragement for any athlete who wants to take their walk with Christ to the next level."

Austin Carr, former NFL wide receiver,
codirector of Athletes in Action New Orleans

GLORIFYING GOD IN SPORTS

THE
CHRISTIAN
ATHLETE

BRIAN SMITH

DAVID C COOK

transforming lives together

THE CHRISTIAN ATHLETE
Published by David C Cook
4050 Lee Vance Drive
Colorado Springs, CO 80918 U.S.A.

Integrity Music Limited, a Division of David C Cook
Brighton, East Sussex BN1 2RE, England

The graphic circle C logo is a registered trademark of David C Cook.

The website addresses recommended throughout this book are offered as a
resource to you. These websites are not intended in any way to be or imply an
endorsement on the part of David C Cook, nor do we vouch for their content.

Details in some stories have been changed to protect
the identities of the persons involved.

Library of Congress Control Number 2021943997
ISBN 978-0-8307-8325-0
eISBN 978-0-8307-8326-7

The Team: Michael Covington, Stephanie Bennett, Jeff Gerke, Judy
Gillispie, James Hershberger, Susan Murdock, Angela Messinger
Cover Design: James Hershberger
Cover Photo: Getty Images

Printed in the United States of America
First Edition 2022

1 2 3 4 5 6 7 8 9 10

120121

Contents

Introduction

"God, what do you even want from me as an athlete?"

I wish I would have asked that question and listened for a response instead of just telling him what *I* wanted when it came to my sport.

I recited one Bible verse before every cross-country race in high school and college. And no, it wasn't Philippians 4:13. I figured everyone else was using that one so I would try something different in an attempt to stand out.

Besides, I prayed the "Philippians prayer" (*I can do all things through Christ!*) during basketball season. Distance running deserved a running verse.

My pre-race prayer came from Isaiah:

> They who wait for the LORD shall renew their
> strength;
> they shall mount up with wings like
> eagles;
> they shall run and not be weary;
> they shall walk and not faint. (40:31)

It's hard to tell if God ever answered the prayer the way I hoped. Racing never felt easy, and my legs often felt like I was carrying a rhinoceros as the finish line approached. That's a far cry from the experience of mounting an eagle, whatever that's supposed to mean.

The truth is, I never fully understood what God wanted from me when it came to applying my faith to my sport. Praying before competition seemed like a good start. But what else did God want from me?

I'm guessing you're reading this because you're asking yourself a similar question: *How do I integrate my faith with my sport? How do I do this sport in a way that honors God?*

The purpose of this book is to answer that question. I've written this from a biblical perspective aimed at helping you glorify Jesus Christ in every facet of your sport.

This book is for you, the athlete. Not your coach. Not your parents. Not your fans. Athlete, consider this book an assist from me to you.

With that being said, though, I know others involved in sports can benefit from what's laid out in this book. That list includes but is not limited to coaches, athletic directors, athletic administrators, and parents of kids involved in sport. If that's you, I'm going to refer to you as "coach." At the end of each chapter, after reflection questions for athletes, I provide additional ones for coaches to work through.

Speaking of coaches, in this book I sometimes refer to the darker side of coaching. In no way am I insinuating that *all* coaches act in those ways.

My aim in *The Christian Athlete* is to biblically shape the way you think about your sport and present a practical approach to having a God-centered perspective for every challenge the world of athletics throws at you. I rely heavily on the Word of God and my own experience both as a former competitive athlete and as a coach who has been working with and discipling college athletes since 2006.

The first chapter addresses what God ultimately wants from us.

After laying the groundwork, we'll look through the different circumstances brought about by sports and seek to understand how we can glorify God in each of them. We will explore potentially new ways of experiencing, appreciating, and practicing obedience to God in the middle of all the circumstances athletes face—motivation, pressure, winning, losing, injuries, practice, teammates, riding the bench, gray areas, coaches, and retirement.

Finally, we'll see how the mission and platform afforded to athletes offer a unique opportunity to spread the gospel. With that in mind, I'll give you practical training to leverage your privileged position for the glory of God and the advancement of his kingdom.

 How do I integrate my faith with my sport? How do I do this sport in a way that honors God?

We need to learn to make our sport something that draws us closer to God. We were created with a longing that cannot be filled by anything or anyone but God. There will always be a ceiling on the amount of happiness earthly things can bring us, and more often than not, we will be disappointed at how low that ceiling is.

That will be a continual theme of this book. Sports are a good gift from God to us to enjoy, but we can't expect something from them—like soul-filling joy and contentment—that God never intended. Only he can provide those eternal longings inside us.

Ecclesiastes 3:11 says that God has put eternity in our hearts. The implication is simple: we cannot be satisfied by earthly things. When we use our sport to get more of God, we align ourselves with the way God intended his good gifts, like sports, to work. And in the end, we also get the maximum amount of joy out of our sport. As we grow in our understanding of that, we are freed up to enjoy sports for what they are (a good gift from God) instead of trusting them for what they can never give (ultimate purpose, meaning, and satisfaction).

"God, what do you even want from me as an athlete?" That's the subject of the first chapter.

1

On Glory and God

You keep using that word. I do not think it
means what you think it means.

Iñigo Montoya, *The Princess Bride*

What does God even want from you as an athlete? The same thing
he wants across the entirety of his creation: glory.

In order for you to understand how to integrate your faith into
the sport you compete in, you must first understand this essential
concept. This chapter will provide a brief overview of the doctrine of
glory. We'll quickly get to how to apply it to all aspects of your life
in sports, but it's paramount that we start here.

Author and theologian John Piper shines light on a ground-
breaking biblical truth:

> God's ultimate goal is to preserve and display his
> infinite and awesome greatness and worth, that is,
> his glory.
>
> God has many other goals in what he does. But
> none of them is more ultimate than this. They are all

subordinate. God's overwhelming passion is to exalt
the value of his glory. To that end he seeks to display
it, to oppose those who belittle it, and to vindicate it
from all contempt. It is clearly the uppermost reality
in his affections. He loves his glory infinitely.[1]

Please do not just take Piper's word for it or my own. Look at
what the Bible (God's Word) has to say about it.[2]

- Isaiah 43:6–7—God created us for his glory.
- Jeremiah 13:11—God identifies his purpose for
  calling Israel: his glory.
- Psalm 106:7–8—God rescued Israel from Egypt to
  make known his power.
- Exodus 14:4, 18—God spared Israel from Pharaoh's
  attack for the glory of his name.
- 2 Samuel 7:23—God granted victory to Israel for
  the glory of his name.
- 2 Kings 19:34—Jerusalem was saved for the glory
  of God's name.
- Ezekiel 36:22–23—Israel returned from exile to
  vindicate the glory of his name.
- Habakkuk 2:14—One day God will fill the earth
  with the knowledge of his glory.

Okay, but those were all from the Old Testament. What does
the New Testament have to say?

- John 7:18—Jesus sought the glory of God in his actions.
- Matthew 5:16—Our good works bring glory to God.
- John 14:13—God is glorified through our answered prayers.
- John 12:27–28; 17:1—Jesus' motivation for enduring suffering was God's glory.
- John 17:24—Jesus' desire for us is to see and enjoy his glory.
- Ephesians 1:4–6, 12, 14—God chose his people for his glorious grace.
- 1 Corinthians 10:31—We are implored to do everything for God's glory.
- 1 Peter 4:11—We should serve in a way that brings glory to God.

Get the picture? God is infinitely passionate about his glory. You probably already knew that on some level. My guess, though, is that your knowledge was probably based more on cultural norms than biblical conviction. After all, everybody—especially athletes—knows you are supposed to "give glory to God."

But what does that mean? If you can't give a clear answer to that question, you need to keep reading.

Before we can really understand what God means by *glory*, we must first see how *our* understanding of *glory*, especially in sports, is often wrong.

Glory ... and Other Words We Don't Understand

I have a good friend who heard a word his freshmen year of college and thought two things:

1. That sounds funny!
2. I'm going to start using it.

This friend made this particular word a regular part of his vocabulary and spent the better part of his freshmen year using it at practice, parties, Christian events, and in everyday conversation. What was the word?

Mofo.

This friend soon found out that it sounded even better when you put the word *crazy* in front of it.

He was ignorant as to what this meant, and it was not until someone lovingly pulled him aside and informed him what he was actually saying when he called people "crazy mofos" that he finally stopped using it.

While it sounded humorous to him, this friend had unintentionally offended many people.

Here's the thing: we make a similar error with the word *glory*.

I think very few of us know what glory is and what it looks like to give it to God. My fear is that "glory to God" has become such a well-rehearsed line by well-meaning, Christ-following athletes that we have become ignorant as to what it actually means or how to recognize it. We throw it around mechanically—knowing we are supposed to say it but unaware of its significance.

As a result, we may be unintentionally offending the infinite God of the universe. It can be very foolish to use a word without understanding its full depth, especially one as important as *glory*.

Though inadvertent, our ignorance surrounding the word *glory* can potentially lead us into three treacherous traps. By no means is this an attempt to pigeonhole every Christian athlete who has ever used the phrase "glory to God." These are dangers we can fall prey to, however, when we have a distorted view of glory.

Danger #1: Prideful Redirection

We've all seen it plenty of times. An athlete makes a fantastic play. The crowd goes crazy. The athlete celebrates with his or her teammates. After the game, the interview follows a predictable script:

> Media: "Can you walk us through the big play you made?"
> Athlete: "I mean, I want to start by giving all the glory to God and thank him for this moment."

This is called redirecting praise. Somebody offers you a compliment and you attempt to deflect praise by giving credit to someone else. What possible danger is there in that?

Acts 14 gives us some insight into this. Paul and Barnabas were in a city called Lystra, and Paul healed a guy who had been unable to walk since birth. Let's begin in verse 11:

> When the crowds saw what Paul had done, they lifted up their voices, saying in Lycaonian, "The

gods have come down to us in the likeness of men!"
Barnabas they called Zeus, and Paul, Hermes,
because he was the chief speaker. And the priest of
Zeus, whose temple was at the entrance to the city,
brought oxen and garlands to the gates and wanted
to offer sacrifice with the crowds. (vv. 11–13)

Athlete, can you recognize what is going on in this scenario?
Let's recap. Paul and Barnabas did something amazing that drew
the attention of the crowd. The crowd went crazy, screaming their
names and comparing them to the all-time greats. Maybe they
even did the wave. This type of behavior happens every week in our
sports-saturated culture.

Paul and Barnabas had a great response. They did not say, "All
the glory to God!" They did not say, "Thanks, guys. We just want
to take a second to thank our Lord and Savior Jesus Christ." They
didn't double-fist pound their chests and point to the sky. Instead,
they ran to the scene and pleaded with the crowd to stop worshipping
them. Paul and Barnabas did not buy into their hype. Even
though the crowd cheered them on, they actively pushed against
the praise.

Paul and Barnabas understood the danger of being praised and
worshipped. That story happened in Acts 14. Just a couple of chapters
earlier, in Acts 12, a man was struck dead by the Lord because
he failed to give God proper glory. Paul and Barnabas show us the
right way to respond to glory that belongs only to God. They aggressively
attacked the praise lavished on them and sought to get the
spotlight off themselves.

Danger #2: Heartless Dedication

The concept here is pretty simple. We tell fans and media that we play our sport to glorify God or as a grateful response for what he has done for us. Many Christian athletes will use the phrase *AO1* (audience of One) as a way of saying they play for God.

If that's truly the case, great! My fear, however, is that Christian athletes can give excellent lip service to the Lord, when in reality our hearts are not centered on God or even thinking about him at all. The "all glory to God" declarations after a game become merely a robotic response—maybe with good intentions but delivered without serious reflection on whether or not what we just did *actually* was glorifying to him.

I am guilty of this many Sundays at church. While singing praise songs, my mind will repeatedly drift toward plans for the rest of the afternoon. Outwardly, I look like a great Christian who is singing to God. But my heart is often disconnected from the words coming out of my mouth. It happens in church—and it happens in sports. If you are claiming to compete for an audience of One but your words aren't backed up by your attitude and your actions, not only during the competition but also through the daily rhythms of your sport, I want to plead with you to please be careful.

Isaiah 1 paints a terrifying picture of how God responds to this kind of hypocrisy. The people of God were offering sacrifices and throwing parties and festivals as prescribed by the law. They were doing and saying all the right things.

But there was a problem.

God was not a fan. In fact, he said he actually hated their religious faking at a soul level (Isa. 1:14).

The people of God had fallen into the dangerous trap of heartless dedication. They were saying the right things. They were even doing some of the right things. If it were today, they probably would be tweeting the right things too. But the connection between their hearts and their hands was severed. Rehearsing the right phrases or words does not score any brownie points with a jealous God who wants more than our lip service.

Danger #3: End Product Over Process

A third danger we can fall prey to when we don't fully understand what glory is and how to give it to God is that we can misunderstand what the Lord really desires from us.

Have you ever noticed the moments when we do or do not give glory to God?

After the game-winning play? Yep.

After a big performance? Yep.

After losing a big game? Nope.

When suffering an injury? Nope.

We wrongly assume that God gets the glory primarily when we win.

Does he want us to play with excellence? Absolutely. I would argue (and I do in chapter 4) that doing so reflects his image very well.

The problem, however, is that we often believe God is more glorified through the person who hit the game-winning shot than through the defender who gave it everything he had but failed. We have made a dangerous link between earthly success and the primary way God is glorified.

Beyond that, we far too often assume that God's glory through sport comes mainly during the game, race, or match itself. Competition is important. And all your training, thinking, and preparation lead to the moment when you risk it all against an opponent. But competition makes up about 1 percent of what you do as an athlete. The other 99 percent of the time is spent practicing, lifting, eating, sleeping, stretching, watching film, practicing again, traveling, and so on.

We have made a dangerous link between earthly success and the primary way God is glorified.

I would spend three months training for a race that took about four minutes to complete. God doesn't want only what we do in competition. He wants everything, including our hearts.

The book of 1 Samuel shows that our hearts are actually the apex of what God is after. God sent Samuel to choose the next king of Israel from among Jesse's sons. Predictably, Jesse brought out the son he thought was the best option. Here's how the scene plays out:

> When they came, he looked on Eliab and thought, "Surely the LORD's anointed is before him." But the LORD said to Samuel, "Do not look on his appearance or on the height of his stature, because I have rejected him. For the LORD sees not as man sees: man looks on the outward appearance, but the LORD looks on the heart." (16:6–7)

In a sports-centered, top-plays culture, we are easily deceived into believing that what impresses us must also impress God. It's an easy mistake to make. But it's not one without consequences.

These three dangers are the result of our wrong assumptions about glory. As was the case with my friend misunderstanding what he was saying, we must have a clear understanding of what we're talking about if we want to give God what he desires most. Glory is literally a weighty concept.

What Is God's Glory?

Glory simply means "weight." It means a particular object is heavy with worth or significance. And the more glory an object has, the more it will affect the environment around it and cause people to notice.

Tim Keller states that *God's* glory is "at least the combined magnitude of all God's attributes and qualities put together."[3] In a sense, Keller is saying that God's glory is the combined weight of everything that makes God *God*. His love, justice, goodness, wrath, omniscience, omnipotence, majesty, wisdom, and grace are all aspects of who he is and, when combined, are "at least" what makes up his glory.

John Piper unpacks God's glory this way:

> What is it? I believe the glory of God is the going
> public of his infinite worth. I define the holiness
> of God as the infinite value of God, the infinite
> intrinsic worth of God. And when that goes public

in creation, the heavens are telling the glory of God, and human beings are manifesting his glory, because we're created in his image, and we're trusting his promises so that we make him look gloriously trustworthy.[4]

If we combine Keller's and Piper's definitions of God's glory, we could conclude that God's glory is at least the weight of everything that makes him God and the declaration of that weight for others to notice.

The big (glorious!) question that remains for athletes is this: *In light of how much glory God already has, how can we possibly give glory to God through our sport?*

What Does It Mean to Give God Glory?

Giving glory to God certainly doesn't mean that we can somehow add to his glory by what we do or say. God is not lacking in glory; in fact, God is not lacking in any good quality. That's a foundational truth that actually frees us from inflated views of our own importance.

To get this concept, it might be helpful to look at how this plays out in sports. Think of LeBron James. When fans chant his name, cheer him on, and, in an odd sense, worship him, they are not making him a better basketball player. He is already an incredible basketball player. When fans cheer for him and talk about his greatness as a basketball player, they are going public with the truth about him so others can know and be affected by it too.

See the difference? He's already a great basketball player, and this is demonstrated by what he does on the court. The fans give him glory by acknowledging his greatness.

So giving God glory means thinking and acting in a way that pleases him and draws attention to who he is. As an athlete, you bring glory to God when you think and act in a way that pleases him and draws attention to who he is.

But who is he?

God as Father

For us to know what God wants, we first need to know who he truly is. This can be difficult, of course. He is infinite, and we are limited. Yet there is much that he has revealed about himself that we can understand.

Paul never penned a letter to the church at Lambeau Field or Madison Square Garden, so we will never fully know how God views athletic achievements, especially those "given" to him. Through the life of Jesus and his many parables, though, we do get a glimpse of how God desires to be seen.

Before Jesus began his public ministry, he was baptized by his cousin, John the Baptist. As he rose from the water, a voice from heaven declared "This is my beloved Son, with whom I am well pleased" (Matt. 3:17). Jesus healed the sick. He raised the dead. He gave sight to the blind. He showed dignity to the undignified. He died for our sins and rose from the dead, giving us access to a restored relationship with God the Father. And before Jesus did any of that, God declared his pleasure over Jesus based on sonship—not performance.

In his classic book *Knowing God*, J. I. Packer answers the question: What is a Christian? "The question can be answered in many ways, but the richest answer I know is that a Christian is one who has God as Father."[5]

This is good news for us not only as Christians but also as Christians who happen to be athletes. God has revealed himself as Father, which is a relational description we're familiar with, even if we've known only imperfect fathers. As a perfect Father, God's primary pleasure with us is grounded in our status as his adopted sons or daughters. But we're not born with that status.

What Is the Gospel?

Before we go any further, we need to make sure we understand the basic gospel message. It's a message that starts with some bad news before getting to the best news the world has ever heard. Much of this book assumes you understand the message below and have based your right standing before God on it. If you have, this should be a good refresher, contextualized to you as an athlete. If you haven't heard this message, this is good news that demands a response.

First Things First

The bad news: We do not enter this world as children of God. None of us do. The Bible actually says we "were by nature children of wrath" (Eph. 2:3).

It gets worse: The gap that separates us from God is caused by our own sin. We are all guilty of it, according to Romans 3:23.

And it gets even worse: Romans 6:23 says we must pay a penalty for our disobedience. "The wages of sin is death."

To sum it up, we are born not as God's children but as objects of his wrath because of our sin. And the price we must pay for that sin is death. That's the bad news.

If we're honest with ourselves, I think we all know that something inside us is ... off. And as athletes, we often want to fix it ourselves. Our athletic mentality says, *I can see where I am weak in a specific area or skill set. So my next step is to work hard at it and get better.* That works in sports. Sometimes it works in life. But when it comes to our relationship with God, no amount of spiritual training or "getting ourselves right" will bring God to say, "Yeah, you're good now."

Athlete, you can't come into relationship with the God of the universe on your own terms. That's the bad news.

So who's ready for some good news?

The word *gospel* actually means "good news," so we'll refer to it as such. Romans 6:23 sounds like doom and gloom, but it's followed by very good news indeed. There is always a *but* with God. In its entirety, the verse reads: "The wages of sin is death, *but* the free gift of God is eternal life in Christ Jesus our Lord."

Because we sin, we deserve death. God sent his Son, Jesus, to the earth. He lived a life without sin and died the death we deserve. Then God raised him from the dead! Jesus' death satisfied the price we owed for our sin.

And it's completely free. That's the definition of *grace*—a free and undeserved gift. This is hard for anyone to wrap their mind around, especially athletes. You work for everything in sports. Nothing is just given to you. There's a passage in Ephesians that helps us understand why God chose this route for relational intimacy with him:

"By grace you have been saved through faith. And this is not your own doing; it is the gift of God, not a result of works, so that no one may boast" (Eph. 2:8–9).

So that no one may boast. God wants the glory.

You become a child of God—a Christian—when you respond to this gift by confessing with your mouth that Jesus is Lord and believing in your heart that God raised him from the dead (Rom. 10:9). If you have never done that before, here is a sample prayer to express the desire of your heart to God:

> God, I know I have sinned and fallen short of your glory. I understand that I can't make things right with you on my own. I need you. God, forgive me. Thank you for your Son, Jesus. I believe he paid the price for my sins on the cross. I believe he rose from the dead. I believe he is my Savior, and I want to make him Lord of my life too. Amen.

If you just expressed those words to God, I'd love to celebrate with you. You can connect with me through social media or my website, TheChristianAthlete.com, and let me know you just became a child of God.

When you do become a child of God, you gain the privilege of calling God your Father. And he gives you his Spirit to help as you walk forward in your new relationship with Jesus. He will never leave you.

Besides desiring his glory, this relational identity shows God's desire for you to enjoy him as Father. C. S. Lewis put it this way: "In commanding us to glorify Him, God is inviting us to enjoy Him."[6] Athlete, God longs for us to find our ultimate satisfaction in him, not to search aimlessly for it through sports.

Against the backdrop of your primary identity as a child of the King, you can begin to glorify him through your secondary identity as an athlete. The order is crucial in how we approach glorifying God through sports.

Being a *Christian* athlete frees us to play, practice, and perform *from* love, not *for* love.

It empowers us to maximize our God-given talent *from* a position of acceptance, not *for* acceptance.

> Against the backdrop of your primary identity as a child of the King, you can begin to glorify him through your secondary identity as an athlete.

Unbiblical Views of God—from the World of Sports

Without a biblical understanding of who God is and how he primarily sees us, we can easily default to an unhealthy view of him that inhibits our ability to fully glorify him.

The narrative we can drift toward believing is that God does not really care about sports. He may care about a lot of things, including us, but he is far too busy to be concerned with something as silly as a game. We imagine that God is concerned only about the platform that sports give us to share his love with other people. The danger of this view of God is that it can ruin your motivation for playing. After all, if he doesn't care, why should you?

We see in the Gospel accounts that God pursues us relentlessly, even sending his Son to die for us. Moreover, the parables and stories, not to mention the rest of the New Testament, portray a God whose interest in us extends far beyond what we might call religious activities to include all of life.

Dr. Ed Uszynski, who has worked with elite athletes for the last three decades at the intersection of faith and sport, wrote:

> A crucified yet victorious Christ should be proof enough that God doesn't operate with the same definitions of winning and losing as humans. But God most certainly does care who wins—just not at all in the same way we do and certainly not in the way implied by most post-game interviews. He cares about everything that happens in the universe. His sovereignty extends to the atomic level, where every atom of every cell arranges itself in relation to every other according to His plans and purposes.[7]

Perhaps Abraham Kuyper summed it up best when he said, "There is not a square inch in the whole domain of our human existence over which Christ, who is Sovereign over all, does not cry 'Mine!'"[8]

The point is that God is not indifferent about anything that takes place within his universe—which includes how you play and how you think about your sport. He cares about every detail of your life as an athlete.

As we continue to consider how sports can drive us closer to God, we need to leave our performance-based mindset in the rear-view mirror. This doesn't mean we should not strive to be the best we can be in our sport, only that competitive excellence is not the only (or even the primary) category God is concerned with when it comes to his glory. We need to start with what God prioritizes above all else: the heart.

Questions for Individual Reflection or Team Study

Did this chapter offer any new insights to you surrounding the word *glory*? If so, what?

Why do you think it's important to have a working definition of that word within the context of sports?

Why does God care so much about getting the glory?

What verses about God getting glory stood out to you? Did any surprise you?

Which of the three dangers most resonates with you? Why?

How did the author define "giving glory to God"?

Why do you think God wants to be viewed as a father?

If God wanted to be viewed as a fan, how would you bring him glory? What about if he were a coach? What if he were an owner? How does seeing him primarily as a father change how you give him glory?

How do you think your relationship, or lack thereof, with your own father impacts how you view God?

Are you a child of God? When did you make that decision to trust Jesus? If you haven't yet, what are some things preventing you from surrendering your life to him?

Additional Questions for Coaches to Consider

In what ways could understanding God's glory change how you interact with athletes?

Do you think God is currently being glorified through the way you coach? Why or why not?

What excites you about glorifying God in your coaching? What gives you hesitation?

Who have you seen best model this idea of "giving God glory"?

How could understanding that you have an opportunity every day to please God through the way you coach bring a new sense of purpose to your role?

Whether you asked for it or not, you play a parental role in the life of athletes. What do you need to do so your athletes see God's characteristics in you? What do you need to stop doing?

If God prioritizes heart posture over performance, how do you model this to your athletes? Is it possible to do both?

2

On Motivation

Christ in me; I am enough.

Helen Maroulis

I believe I know why you play your sport.

My confidence is based on the belief that beneath our lesser motivations, every athlete plays his or her particular sport for the same underlying reason. And if you are like thousands of other Christian athletes, at some point you have probably claimed Philippians 4:13 as a way to gain what you desire most. But Philippians 4:13—"I can do all things through him who strengthens me"—actually promises to deliver far more than we realize. We often claim it with the hope that God will enable us to experience some form of victory through maximum performance. God, however, offers us something much deeper and more satisfying than a short-lived success.

What do you *really* want from your sports experience? When you perform well, what is it about that experience that makes you want to come back for more? When you struggle or fail, what motivates you to either push forward or sink back? Why do you actually play your sport?

Maybe some of the following sentences resonate with your motivations:

- I play because I like winning.
- I play to feel the joy of playing.
- I play to gain my parents' approval.
- I play to experience my coach's approval.
- I play to garner fans' admiration.
- I play to impress the opposite sex.
- I play to make it to the next level.
- I play to impress my friends.

Did any of those strike a chord with you? Have you ever given serious thought to what drives you to play?

Growing up, I played sports to impress others. I loved it when I did well and other people told me how great I was. As a runner, I literally chased after the admiration I sought from my parents, friends, and coaches. At the time, I would have identified impressing others as my primary motivation. I was wrong—there is a deeper motivation that drives us all. Only when we identify that deep-seated motivation can we truly experience joy through our sport and give God the glory he is due.

Where does Philippians 4:13 fit into all this? You may have this verse tattooed somewhere on your body. If you don't, you probably know someone who does.

"I can do all things through him who strengthens me."

What a great verse! I cannot count how many times I prayed this verse as I toed the line for a track race. I claimed this verse as if to say, *God, I know I can win this race because you will give me strength. It says so right in the Bible.*

Let me introduce you to another passage of Scripture. It's actually in the same chapter.

> I rejoiced in the Lord greatly that now at length you have revived your concern for me. You were indeed concerned for me, but you had no opportunity. Not that I am speaking of being in need, for I have learned in whatever situation I am to be content. I know how to be brought low, and I know how to abound. In any and every circumstance, I have learned the secret of facing plenty and hunger, abundance and need. (vv. 10–12)

If I were to ask you to sum up these three verses in a single word, what would that word be? How would you describe what the apostle Paul is trying to say to his readers?

Maybe you would choose the word *contentment.*

Paul is saying that he has learned to be content in every situation. Whether he has a lot of success or a little, whether he is full or hungry, whether he is on top of the world or in the lowest of valleys, he has learned the secret of being content.

How is he able to do this? He provides the answer in the very next verse, which you will recognize: "I can do all things through him who strengthens me."

Is Paul talking about making the winning shot, winning a championship, or setting a new personal best? No. What he's saying, athlete, is that regardless of whether you succeed or fail in your sport—or at anything in life—you can find contentment in Christ. We wrongly claim Philippians 4:13 to help us succeed in sports, but what God is saying in this verse is that we already have everything we could ever need in Christ. More satisfying than gaining people's approval is getting to a place where you no longer need it. That's the real promise of this verse. And it's infinitely better than how we often use it.

> Whether you succeed or fail in your sport—or at anything in life—you can find contentment in Christ.

Our Ultimate Motivation

Are you ready to learn why you really play your sport? I think you play your sport because you are seeking contentment. The quest for that elusive experience is at the bottom of all your hard work and striving for success. That's the dangling carrot in front of the lesser motivations you may have been able to identify.

The lie we believe is that Philippians 4:13 means we can achieve any outcome in our sport because of Christ. We need to combat that lie with the truth that Philippians 4:13 means we can have contentment regardless of the outcome *because of* Christ. There's a huge difference between the two.

The desire for contentment isn't a bad thing. It's a natural human desire. Who doesn't want to be content? The problem comes when we attempt to find contentment through sports achievements (or any other kind of achievements, for that matter). That's a dead-end pursuit that will always leave us wanting more. If we are going to experience any lasting satisfaction through sports, the goal needs to be God himself, not particular outcomes. A game will never deliver true contentment. This doesn't mean sports are bad or a waste of time. It only means they were never intended to satisfy our hearts at the deepest level.

We will always end up disappointed when we try to use created things to find ultimate satisfaction. C. S. Lewis summarized this misdirected pursuit when he said:

> It would seem that Our Lord finds our desires not too strong, but too weak. We are half-hearted creatures, fooling about with drink and sex and ambition when infinite joy is offered us, like an ignorant child who wants to go on making mud pies in a slum because he cannot imagine what is meant by the offer of a holiday at the sea. We are far too easily pleased.[1]

Lewis suggests that instead of giving up on the idea of finding contentment, we should understand that too often we're simply expecting to get it from the wrong things. The beauty of Philippians 4:13 is that it offers us the proper route to reach the destination of contentment. It's right to claim the verse, but only in the pursuit of a deeper joy that transcends our immediate circumstances.

As I said earlier, God has placed eternity in the hearts of humankind (Eccl. 3:11). An eternal void cannot be satisfied by the temporal things of this world. We need an eternal solution to satisfy our hearts. The contentment we long for is not found in a sport, a job, or an experience. It is found in Jesus.

By this point in the book, this concept should not come as a surprise. If God desires glory, our motivation should be to give it to him. We can—and should—use sports as a vehicle to give him glory. Only then will we find a lasting joy that transcends circumstances.

Think of motivation as the steering wheel in your vehicle. When properly aligned, your car will naturally go straight. Conversely, when it is out of alignment even a little, you will inevitably drift off course without even moving the wheel.

In life it does not take much for us to take our focus off God. It's even easier for athletes deep in competition to forget why they're doing what they're doing. For most of us, the last thing we are thinking about in the heat of the moment is how to be properly motivated. We want to win. We want to compete hard and with excellence. We are focused on the game, not on God. But the question of why we compete is often more important than the outcome itself.

What Does This Look Like Practically?

On August 18, 2016, Helen Maroulis defeated Saori Yoshida from Japan to become the first female wrestler from the United States to win an Olympic gold medal. Yoshida was a sixteen-time consecutive world and Olympic gold medalist. She was unbeatable. Until she faced Maroulis.

In the months leading up to the Olympic Games, Maroulis was in a funk. Struggling with anxiety, fear, and a poor self-image, she knew something needed to happen internally to combat the negativity that consumed her thoughts. She began preaching to herself. She used the mantra "Christ is in me; I am enough" as a rallying cry to drown out the voices in her head. She recited it out loud over and over again. She recited it while she practiced. She recited it while competing, clinging to the things that God said are true about her instead of the opinions of others. One of Maroulis's coaches described the internal motivational shift this way: "Helen had given herself permission to lay it all on the line on the biggest stage sports has to offer because her identity was secure. She was enough with or without that medal."[2]

Amazing! With our identity and motivation firmly grounded in Christ, we are not shaken by the outcome of a competition. We become free to compete without the fear of failure. This opens up an entirely new category for Christian athletes to explore: free athletes can still reach the same apex of human achievement as those bogged down by the incessant need for others' approval.

It's important to note that coming to the point of inner contentment does not mean we let up in competition. Quite the opposite. Using Helen as an example, satisfaction in who Christ says we are gives us the green light to keep pushing forward. The drive to succeed, improve, and win is fueled by knowing the outcome of the competition doesn't change our primary identity as God's children who are *already* fully loved and accepted.

But it's easy to get distracted and fall prey to the trap of idolatry, expecting our sport to deliver things it can't, like long-term satisfaction. When this happens, we worship not God but sport. Paul David Tripp has this to say about worship:

We have been designed by God to be worshippers. This means that worship is our first identity before it ever becomes an activity. The worship inclination or motivation that resides in all our hearts was placed there to draw us to God, the One to whom we were made to give our worship. There is no such thing as a non-worshipping human being. The only thing that divides human beings is what or whom they worship.[3]

In light of this, we need to daily retrain our minds to focus on God so our motivation—and worship—is properly aligned, for God's glory and our own joy.

You need a focal point. A focal point can be anything—a wristband, a tattoo, a watch, something written on your shoes. It could be a scoreboard or banner hung somewhere in the stadium. Ideally, this focal point will be something you consistently see in practice and during competitions.

In his *Handbook on Athletic Perfection*, Wes Neal helps explain how focal points can be a useful tool for Christian athletes. Neal describes a focal point as something you can quickly concentrate on that realigns your focus on your ultimate motivation to glorify God.[4]

When I competed, I would write a Bible verse on my running shoes. As I laced up my shoes before every practice and competition, I would see the verse and it would realign my thoughts to God. It was my daily reminder to bring my Father into those moments when I was naturally inclined to leave him out.

In addition to the challenge of actually remembering God when we participate in our sports, there is the challenge of finding the appropriate time to do so.[5] For a wrestler, the time to realign your motivation is not when you are circling your opponent. For a football player, what happens mentally before the snap has a direct correlation to the play itself. So it's probably not the right time to realign your thoughts to God when you should be analyzing the opponent's formation. A golfer should give 100 percent of his or her focus to determining the break and speed of a particular putt.

No matter your sport, the best time to leverage the effectiveness of a focal point is when there is a pause in the action. Between races, quarters, rounds, or periods is a good time. This will probably be uncomfortable at first. But like anything, the more practice and attention you give to it, the more comfortable you will become using your focal point to realign your motivation.

This can be a new and challenging concept for some athletes to apply. Perhaps you have trained your mind only to zero in on the competition itself, blocking out everything else. As Christians, however, we are called to a higher standard than that. Focal points give us a practical way to move closer to that standard.

Questions for Individual Reflection or Team Study

When have you felt most content in your sport?

Be real: What motivates you to play your sport? What's your why?

How would you define *contentment*?

Read Philippians 4:10–13. How does the whole passage help shape your understanding of verse 13?

What are some new ways you can claim this verse in the context of sports (instead of "I can win/succeed because of Christ")?

Does your story resonate at all with Helen Maroulis's? If so, how?

What is your focal point? If you don't have one yet, what focal point could you make? How can you uniquely leverage that focal point within the context of the sport you play?

Additional Questions for Coaches to Consider

What was your original motivation for getting into coaching? Has that changed over time? If so, how?

The reality for most coaches is "lose and you're fired." So how do you balance that earthly reality *and* find your motivation in glorifying God? Do you think a motivation to win and a motivation to glorify God can complement each other? Why or why not?

How could it help you to recognize the various internal motivations going on in your heart at any given moment?

How do we know when our motivation for coaching becomes more self-serving than God-honoring?

3

On Pressure

Ignoring our emotions is turning our back on reality; listening
to our emotions ushers us into reality. And reality is where
we meet God.... Emotions are the language of the soul.

Dan Allender and Tremper Longman, *The Cry of the Soul*

From the outside, Maddy seemed to have everything going for her. She was an elite athlete, having competed in track and soccer in high school. She'd gone on to run at the University of Pennsylvania. She was smart. She was beautiful. She was well liked by anyone who interacted with her. Her family loved her—and she loved them. Maddy's social media pages presented the image of a young woman who epitomized what a young female athlete should aspire to become.

But on the evening of January 17, while a freshman at UPenn, Maddy Holleran jumped off the ninth floor of a parking garage, instantly killing herself.

What happened to Maddy?

She was depressed, and though her symptoms didn't always exhibit themselves to others around her, something changed in her brain chemistry.

One of her best friends began to sense a change in Maddy after the fall semester. Over Christmas break, Maddy had talked with her friend Emma and Emma's mom around the kitchen table. They had asked her: "Why are you not as happy as you used to be?" and "Can you tell us how you're feeling?"

In an ESPN article titled "Split Image," Kate Fagan notes that:

> Madison was unable to identify exactly what had cast her adrift. Was it the disappointment with Penn, once her dream school? Was she homesick? Was track overwhelming her?
>
> And the most pressing thought of all: If she quit, wasn't she just a failure? Wouldn't that be the first in what would become a lifetime of letdowns?
>
> Madison had always struggled to handle even garden-variety failure. She chased perfection.[1]

Is chasing perfection bad? I don't think so. But if someone's life begins to crumble around her under the weight of the pressures to attain it, the chase is not only bad, it's dangerous.

Chasing perfection and fear of failure are struggles common to athletes. But a deeper look behind the curtain revealed something more going on with Maddy: she struggled with what is now commonly understood as a mental illness.

To me, *mental illness* used to mean this: a middle-aged dude, with ripped and dirty clothes and way too much facial hair, walking down the middle of the street talking to himself. But Maddy didn't check any of those boxes. In fact, from the outside, she represented the polar opposite of what I just described. That's one of the problems with stereotypes: it is not only who they include, but also who they leave out.

We need to understand that mental illness is more than a diagnosis or label insinuating someone should be institutionalized. Mental illness among athletes usually means that our experience with our sport, our relationships, and ourselves becomes increasingly negative. And as the negativity compounds, our risk of collapsing under it increases too.

Before we go any further, I need to give a few disclaimers.

- I am not a trained mental health professional or anywhere close to being an expert.
- My wife specializes in leadership development within our ministry with a specialization in mental health, so through my conversations with her I understand the complexities of the issues enough to give an elementary introduction.
- My purpose in this chapter is to encourage you to take seriously the pressures you face in your sport and life, because God cares deeply about our hearts and minds.
- Please don't take my silence on the benefits and potential solutions available through modern medicine as a sign that I think mental health is solely a spiritual issue that can be "cured" by God.

We will cover three terms in this chapter surrounding the topic of mental health:

1. Mental health—the brain's ability to function.
2. Mental illness—"genetic or circumstantial factors causing a disruption in the brain and affecting a person's thoughts, moods, behaviors, and relationships."[2]
3. Pressure—any stressor in our environment that impacts our mental health. Left unchecked, pressure has the potential to contribute to mental illness.

If *motivation* is the unseen reason for doing something, *pressure* is the unseen reality causing unwanted friction for your motivation. All of us experience pressure. And for the athlete, especially, there is no shortage of it.

Think through everything you're feeling right now that you would classify as a stressor. Seriously, count them up.

How many did you come up with? I bet you didn't count 640. And yet a 2019 study of more than five thousand elite athletes showed "640 distinct stressors that could induce mental health symptoms and disorders."[3]

In the sports culture, we don't talk about these kinds of pressures. Athletes are supposed to be strong. They eat pressure for breakfast. There is no space for negative or hard emotions unless they can be manipulated as fuel for motivation.

Maybe you've heard of the motivational anthem "Nobody cares, work harder."[4]

We need a better solution than this because it's not working. "Nobody cares, work harder" didn't work for Maddy Holleran. It didn't work for Washington State quarterback Tyler Hilinski, who took his own life a few weeks after leading his team to a bowl victory.[5] It's not working for one out of four athletes reporting clinically relevant levels of depressive symptoms.[6] And it's not working for the thousands of athletes feeling crushed under the weight of the pressure.

There is a better path forward. Unsurprisingly, it involves a God who cares about the unseen realities of our souls and also involves his Word, which invites us into an authentic relationship with him.

Athlete, God knows all about you and cares deeply for you. He knows you better than your coach, your teammates, your parents, and your friends know you. He knows you better than you know yourself. You could study all the game film of your life and never fully understand yourself at the level God does.

Pressure and mental health challenges are hardly new categories for a God who has seen it all. And athletes don't hold a monopoly on unhealthy responses to pressure either. The Bible is full of examples of men and women who meet the criteria of undiagnosed mental illness because of the stress they faced.

- Saul wrestled with feelings of worthlessness, excessive guilt, and suicidal ideation (1 Sam. 10:22; 18:8; 31:4).[7]
- David experienced depressive moods, insomnia, fatigue, and a diminished ability to concentrate (Ps. 6:6–7; 13:2; 22:2; 102:7; 2 Sam. 11:2; 13:21).[8]

- Gomer sought adulterous relationships to meet her needs, exhibited relational and emotional instability, and had issues with her identity (Hos. 2:5–12; 6:4).[9]
- Jacob had a long bout of depression and self-destructive behavior (Gen. 37:35; 43:8, 10).[10]
- Job found himself in a persistent negative emotional state of depression, shame, and fear (Job 3:24; 4:5; 6:2–3; 7:3–4).[11]
- Samson was overly impulsive and easily irritated, and he died by suicide (Judg. 14:2, 19; 15:5, 8; 16:26–30).[12]

How we handle the thoughts and emotions swirling around inside us—the pressures we face—is important to God.

When pressed to single out the greatest commandment, Jesus replied in Matthew 22:37 that it is the instruction to love the Lord your God with all your heart and with all your soul and with all your mind.

How we handle the thoughts and emotions swirling around inside us—the pressures we face—is important to God.

That's why we must think better about the pressures in our lives and how we respond—or don't respond to them. Because while the way you steward your heart, soul, and mind may not matter to your coaches (though a lot of them actually do care about these areas of your life), and though it may not be reflected on the scoreboard (though a healthy mind should lead to a higher-performing athlete), it matters to God.

So what does it look like to glorify God by how we handle pressure?

I think it starts by answering two important questions:

1. What are the current pressures you are facing?
2. What tools can you utilize to improve your thought patterns and emotions?

Identify the Pressures You Are Facing

I'm consistently shocked by how little I know about the inner workings of my phone and laptop, despite using them the majority of the day. For instance, did you know we can't connect to the internet without an IP address (Internet Protocol address)? Each device we own has a unique IP address, kind of like a fingerprint. It locates our devices and identifies them to the larger network. The IP address unlocks our device's ability to function at a maximized level by allowing us to connect to the world around us.

Most of us spend countless hours online without thinking twice about what our IP address is and how it's allowing us to engage in the digital world with others. That's fine when we are dealing with the inner workings of our technology. So long as it works, we really don't care. But similar ignorance is not okay when we are dealing with the inner workings of the heart and mind.

I want to introduce you to another IP address that has a significant impact on the way you experience the world around you as an athlete. It's called your "inner pressure address." This IP address is completely unique to you, and it fluctuates based on the environment you're in and the circumstances you experience.

Remember, athletes face 640 potential stressors. The ones you are wrestling with right now and the intensity with which you experience them make up your unique IP address as an athlete.

Nobody else can determine this for you. It's your responsibility to identify the pressures around you. Yes, trained professionals can help you in this area, but you are the one who has to identify what's going on inside you.

Everybody has an IP address. We all have multiple stressors confronting us at any given moment. Pressure itself is not bad or unhealthy. But when it's left unchecked, it can lead to unhealthy thoughts, emotions, and actions.

Why does this matter?

Because there is a direct correlation between rising levels of pressures and mental illness.[13] And identifying them is the first step to stripping them of their power over you.

Here are a couple of questions aimed at identifying the inner pressures you face:

1. Are you struggling with anxiety (excessive fear or worry disproportionate to a given situation) or depression (persistent sadness and a loss of interest in activities you normally enjoy) that interferes with your ability to carry out daily activities and lasts for at least two weeks?

2. Have you experienced any of the following in a way
   that inhibits your ability to complete your normal
   daily routines?
   - low self-esteem (feelings of worthlessness, a
     sense of not being able to do anything right, or
     placing a low value on self)
   - eating concerns
   - sleeping troubles
   - low energy
   - depression
   - anxiety
   - fear of failure
   - perfectionism
   - flashbacks
   - anger outbursts
   - obsessive thoughts and actions
   - attention issues

You glorify God when you show an increased awareness and
ability to identify what is going on inside you. Why? Because, as
we'll learn more about in chapter 10, we serve a God who delights in
order, not chaos. And I truly believe that the order he desires extends
beyond the world around us and into our minds as well.

Knowing your inner pressures is the first step toward peace
because it identifies what needs attention. It's the same reason we
as athletes get X-rays and MRIs when we have pain. Identifying the
what and where of the pain puts us on the path to recovery.

But simply knowing a bone is broken doesn't fix it. In the same way, we need to move beyond just knowledge of our inner pressure's effects on us.

Tools to Train Your Mind

In an article addressed to the collegiate athletic community regarding possible solutions in the area of mental health, Russ Rausch (founder of Vision Pursue) and Ginger Gilmore Childress (Director of Behavioral Medicine, University of Alabama) said:

> Stress and pressure in college athletics and the world appear to be ever increasing. However, you're not helpless. Good solutions to help people cope with and even reduce stress have emerged. When you improve automatic thoughts and emotions, not only do you enhance mental wellness; you give people the best chance to improve performance at the same time.[14]

The mind is like a muscle that can be strengthened. Passivity with our minds will lead to the same results. If we want to reduce our inner pressure in a way that glorifies God, we need increased intentionality in two areas: vulnerability and mental training.

Vulnerability

Think about a balloon. A balloon is created to be filled with air. When we force air into a balloon, pressure begins to build inside, causing the balloon to expand outward. Now, not all balloons are created equal. Some can withstand enormous amounts of pressure before popping, others only a little.

We're similar.

God created us with a unique ability to handle the pressures of life around us. But each of us is also unique in the amount of pressure we can withstand—due to our God-given dispositions and life experiences. This ability to withstand stressors and live in an optimal zone of functioning is also referred to as your "window of tolerance."

Do you know how to release pressure from a balloon? Sure, you can pop it. But that can be a loud and unpleasant process. Another option is to open it back up. The more you open it or the longer you leave it open, the more pressure is released from the inside.

Do you know one potential way to lower your IP address? Open yourself up to someone you trust and tell that person about the stressors you're feeling. Perhaps more relief would come from finding a group of trusted people with whom you can practice authenticity and vulnerability.

I struggled with habitual sin while I was in college. Sensing its increasing power over me, I finally called my girlfriend at the time (now my wife) and told her about my struggle. That was the first step on a path to freedom for me. I wasn't cured overnight. But the sin lost its power over me when it became public.

Sin festers and grows in the dark. It's why the Bible tells us in James 5:16 to confess our sins to one another. Though the inner pressure we are facing is not sin, I think a similar approach is needed.

Nothing good comes when it lingers in the dark, even if it's not inherently sinful. Ignoring the pressures you face or burying them inside will not bring you relief and contentment. At best, the weight of the pressure will hinder your performance in competition. At worst, it will suck the joy out of your sport—and potentially your life.

Let's not overcomplicate what this looks like practically.

If it's the night before a competition and you are feeling pressure that's preventing you from sleeping, just text or call a friend. A simple "Hey, I can't stop thinking about tomorrow—can you pray for me right now?" might be all it takes. If you're involved in a team Bible study, don't be ashamed to ask your teammates to pray for you about the areas where you feel unhealthy amounts of pressure. I know some people get relief from journaling. Journaling amounts to vulnerability with yourself or, if you write it as a prayer journal, vulnerability with God.

The most mentally unhealthy athletes I have worked with are the ones who neglect to acknowledge the pressures they are facing to self, others, and God.

Admitting the areas of our lives that cause us unwanted stress may feel like an act of weakness, especially in an athletic culture that celebrates a "nobody cares, work harder" mentality. But it's quite the opposite. It shows incredible strength, courage, and bravery to share about your struggles with someone else.

Before Jesus went to the cross, he spent time with his Father, praying through his thoughts about what was to come. He was raw. He was honest. I think one reason Jesus modeled this for us was to give us permission and encouragement to do likewise—before God and before others.

Ultimately, ignoring the realities of the pressures we face is a refusal to glorify and love God with all our hearts, souls, and minds. Vulnerability is the path to freedom and joy.

In his book *Hope in the Dark*, Craig Groeschel put it this way:

> We're afraid to say what we're feeling, deep down in the dark corners of our souls. We're terrified that if we admit how we're feeling, then our faith will crack. But the opposite is true. It's when we suppress the pain of what we're experiencing, stuffing it down and denying it, that our faith becomes so hard and brittle that it breaks.[15]

Mental Training

When I was in elementary school, I entered a free throw shooting competition. After winning a few local and regional tournaments, I made it to the state finals. In what would (unfortunately) be the apex of my basketball career, I took fourth place overall.

Each shot was the same. Three dribbles while I quietly recited Philippians 4:13—completely out of context, by the way. *"I can do all things through Christ who strengthens me."* Spin ball with two hands while envisioning the ball swishing through the net. Find the seams on the ball without looking at it. Bend my knees. Then, shoot. Most of the time, it would go in.

Free throw shooting is about focus. It's about rhythm and habits. The worst enemy of someone shooting a free throw is distraction. That's why home teams are silent when their player is at the free throw line and scream when the opponent is shooting.

Many athletes have adopted the art of visualizing themselves succeeding in their sport. We do it because it works. And it works outside of athletics too.

At its core, it's meditation. But if you're like me, that word stirs up an image of someone sitting cross-legged on a yoga mat with his thumbs pressed against his fingers, on top of a mountain while watching the sunset. I want to rebrand meditation—which is actually a biblical concept—and call it *mental training* for the rest of the chapter.

Studies and anecdotal evidence consistently show a link between appropriate mental training and decreased stress and anxiety.[16] If stressors in our lives increase our inner pressures, then mental training can be seen as a fight for inner peace.

It's important to note that if we want to glorify God through a pursuit of positive mental health, we need to do it God's way. Mental training in pursuit of God's peace (which he wants us to have, by the way) involves filling our minds, not emptying them. And what do we fill our minds with?

His Word.

- Psalm 1:1–2 shows us that the blessed man is one who delights himself in God's Word and meditates on it day and night.
- In Psalm 119:148, David mentions staying up late at night to meditate on God's promises.
- Psalm 143:5 says, "I remember the days of old; I meditate on all that you have done; I ponder the work of your hands."

What if we began to use his Word as a weapon for our minds instead of as a misguided ploy to pursue a win? Athlete, one of the best ways to reduce the stress in your life is to memorize Scripture. God's Word allows us to see reality through his lens instead of through our own skewed perception. It allows us to recalibrate our minds toward what is true.

> In the battle for our mental health, God's Word can be the bridge that allows us to move from pressure to peace.

If you sense the inner pressure in your life rising, I would encourage you to have these verses readily available:

> Do not be anxious about anything, but in everything by prayer and supplication with thanksgiving let your requests be made known to God. And the peace of God, which surpasses all understanding, will guard your hearts and your minds in Christ Jesus. Finally, brothers, whatever is true, whatever is honorable, whatever is just, whatever is pure, whatever is lovely, whatever is commendable, if there is any excellence, if there is anything worthy of praise, think about these things. (Phil. 4:6–8)

Take your inner pressures to God. "Take every thought captive to obey Christ" (2 Cor. 10:5b). He desires to give you the kind of peace you cannot attain apart from him.

In the battle for our mental health, God's Word can be the bridge that allows us to move from pressure to peace.

Questions for Individual Reflection or Team Study

How comfortable are you talking about mental health? What has contributed to your perspective?

How do you feel knowing that God knows more about you than you do and that he cares deeply about how you steward your heart and mind?

How did you answer the set of questions aimed at identifying your "personal IP address" in this chapter?

What are your next steps, either personally or as a team?

What will it look like for you to reflect regularly on your personal IP address?

Additional Questions for Coaches to Consider

On a scale of 1–10, how aware are you of your athletes' mental health?

Do you think better understanding your athletes' mental health allows you to serve them better as athletes and as individuals? Why or why not?

Who on your team is responsible for collecting local resources for mental health?

How can you go about sharing those resources with your team?

What are the current inner pressures you face in your role?

4

On Winning

Sport doesn't work if we don't care.

Dr. Brian Bolt, *Sport. Faith. Life.*

We need a better theology surrounding the topic of winning. There are too many questions and not enough answers. Is it okay for me to want to win? How does a Christian athlete approach the topic of winning? How much should an athlete care about it? At what point does an athlete cross over to the idol-infested waters of caring too much? Does God care if we pray for a win or for success? Can God be glorified through winning? If so, how? Is God glorified *only* when we win?

This chapter will not answer all these questions, but I hope it will move the ball forward in our understanding of how we should think about winning in light of Scripture. We'll start by addressing some common errors.

Error #1: Being Humble in Victory Means Not Celebrating

I was a D1 track/cross-country runner, but I also have played golf recreationally since I was fifteen. To this day, I have not gotten any better, yet there is something about playing a game that is impossible to beat that continues to lure me back. On one particular fall day in Michigan, I learned that while you cannot beat the game, you can conquer individual holes.

I skulled it. At least that's what one of my friends told me as I watched my ball skip through the grass on the way to the green. It was a 143-yard par 3. I had a new set of Nike knockoff clubs, and I went with an 8 iron. The green sat above the tee box, so you couldn't tell if your shot made it up and settled nicely on the green or if it rolled off the back. Sand traps were situated on both sides of the green, inviting disaster.

There are few better feelings in the world of sport than hitting a golf ball cleanly and crisply, exactly as you envision it before lining up your shot. This was not one of those moments. As my club moved through its downward trajectory, I felt my error before I saw it. The cold weather, combined with the reverberating steel shaft of the club, did no favors to my wimpy hands.

"Skulled it, huh?" my buddy remarked as the rest of the peanut gallery that made up my friends laughed. A skulled shot is when the front edge of the club face strikes the middle of the golf ball. The result is a ball that comes off the club fast and flat, with little to no spin and even less distance control. It's a horrible-looking shot.

"Yep, that sucks," I replied, all the while trying to play it cool and not give them the satisfaction of knowing I hurt my hands in the process.

After resisting the urge to hit a mulligan (nobody likes to hit a bad shot, especially on a par 3), I hopped into the golf cart and drove up the hill to the green to survey the damage. I have a bad habit of not watching where my shot goes, especially when I don't hit it well.

We arrived at the green to see three balls scattered around the putting surface and, predictably, my ball was not one of them. I went to the back of the green and started searching through the trees and bushes. Nothing. My three friends left their spot on the green and, out of pity, helped me look.

"Did you check the hole?" My friend snickered as he made his way back to the pin.

I wasn't going to satisfy him with a response.

"Brian."

"Shut up," I said.

"Are you [censored] kidding me?"

I looked up. As I did, he yanked the pin out of the hole. My ball popped out with it.

A hole in one! I wish I had video evidence of the chaos that ensued as we all celebrated. The worst shot of the day ended up being the best shot of my life. As I replayed the shot and the events leading up to the revelation that my ball somehow found its way into the hole, I thought to myself, *It sure was great that my friends were part of it.*

That led me to another question: What would it have felt like if nobody had been there to witness it? Would it still have been great? Sure. But would it have been as great as it was? I don't think so. How would I have experienced that moment if I hadn't celebrated it?

I was reminded that day that joy is maximized when we can share it with others. That's part of how God designed us. When things happen in isolation, there is a cap on our enjoyment of it. The celebration we had together on the golf course that day helped me understand another way sports can contribute to God's glory and our enjoyment.

Celebration completes the highs we experience in sports. C. S. Lewis helped me discover this amazing truth in his book *Reflections on the Psalms*:

> I think we delight to praise what we enjoy because the praise not merely expresses but completes the enjoyment; it is its appointed consummation. It is not out of compliment that lovers keep on telling one another how beautiful they are; the delight is incomplete till it is expressed.[1]

Imagine accomplishing something great in your sport and not having the opportunity to express it outwardly or have someone to share it with. That lack would certainly lessen the experience. This is true across all categories of life. It's why we love social media. When something good happens to us, we can hardly hold it in. Sharing becomes an extension of the experience. So we tweet. We post. We snap. We text.

Celebrating good things that happen to us is not evidence of lack of humility; it is part of how God designed us to react. Obviously, when the overflow of our joy takes the form of taunting our opponent, a line has been crossed and the legitimate expression of celebration quickly devolves into a lack of humility. I trust you know the difference between the two. The point is this: our God is a joy optimizer!

So when you experience a victory, don't be afraid to celebrate it. Dance with your teammates; hug your coach; give yourself permission and freedom to experience the emotion of happiness (just be sure to do it with class). God has given you your gift and sport to glorify him, and one way you can do that is by just enjoying the fun moments your sport brings to you.

Error #2: Winning Will Finally Make You Happy

Whether or not he is the greatest quarterback of all time, Tom Brady is at least in the discussion. Apart from his tremendous success on the football field, he has quite a few other things going for him. He's handsome, has a supermodel wife, and has more money than he knows what to do with. Why, then, did he say the following in a 2005 interview with *60 Minutes*?

> Why do I have three Super Bowl rings and still think there's something greater out there for me? I mean, maybe a lot of people would say, "Hey, man, this is what is." I reached my goal, my dream, my life. Me, I think, *God, it's got to be more than this.* I mean, this can't be what it's all cracked up to be. I mean, I've done it. I'm twenty-seven. And what else is there for me?[2]

When asked what the answer was, Brady, with a hint of desperation in his voice, responded, "I wish I knew. I wish I knew."

Our culture has no answer for Brady's question, though everyone is secretly asking it. His response goes against our culture's core promise—that we can find happiness in things or experiences.

You are not Tom Brady. Your success may be simply making the team. Or finishing in eighth place but still beating your personal best by a few seconds. Athlete, you do not need to be at an elite level to live in a destructive cycle that leaves you wanting more.

It's a never-ending spiral that goes something like this:

1. You compete.
2. You win or succeed.
3. It feels good.
4. A short while later, the high is gone, and you need to do it all over again.

Winning gives you a taste of joy, acceptance, and satisfaction, but you want more. This is not surprising to God. He created you in his image, and you are hardwired so that earthly satisfaction will never fulfill you. Sports are wonderful, but they are not ultimate. They cannot satisfy your heart at the deepest level.

> Athlete, you do not need to be at an elite level to live in a destructive cycle that leaves you wanting more.

Solomon wrote the book of Ecclesiastes, a book dedicated to lamenting the fact that true joy cannot be found in the pleasures this earth offers. The Bible does not say whether King Solomon could throw a baseball or read a zone defense. We do know that he was good-looking.[*] He was rich.[†] He was strong.[‡] It's not hard to

---

[*] 1 Samuel 9:2
[†] 9:1
[‡] 9:2

imagine women being drawn to him. On paper, he had it all. And yet he wrestled with the same issue that Tom Brady and many other athletes wrestle with.

Sports can give us some amazing highs, but we come crashing back down to earth a short while later. Winning is great, and we should desire to pursue it, but there is a good reason it doesn't satisfy us at a soul level. It was never supposed to. We were created for more. We were created for eternity.

Error #3: The Only Thing That Matters Is Your Effort on Game Day

When you've worked to become excellent at what you do, you bring honor to the One who created you and gave you that particular skill set (Prov. 22:29; 1 Cor. 10:31). We often throw around this line: "All God cares about is you giving your best." It has become the consolation prize for losing. It's yet another product of our everyone-gets-a-trophy culture. Does God care if you give your best? Absolutely. When athletes give less than their best, they fall short of their calling to steward their gifts to the best of their abilities.

The problem with that line is the word *all*. It suggests that God cares *only* about your effort and nothing else. So don't worry if you stink. Don't worry if you were not fully present mentally or if you didn't prepare. Don't worry if you ignored your coaches. He's not concerned with your skill level, only how hard you try during the competition itself.

The problem is that we often limit "giving our best" to our performance on game day. If you are habitually lazy in practice, in the weight room, and with your eating and sleeping habits, and then you give 100 percent during the competition, is that really your best? Does that kind of effort glorify God? Colossians 3:23 encourages us to do *everything* as if we were doing it for the Lord. That would seem to include the way we prepare for competition.

 Effort is not the same as excellence.

Imagine a person who felt that practicing his faith consisted entirely of giving his all for one hour each Sunday. No prayer, no Bible study, and no service the rest of the week. Would that kind of faith glorify God?

Or what if the ark that Noah built was littered with holes? Would God say, "Well, he sure isn't very good at shipbuilding, but I did notice that he was sweating a lot and giving it a good effort. It's going to sink, but at least he tried." I doubt God would say that.

God didn't tell Noah merely to build a boat. God gave Noah very specific instructions on how to build that boat, and he expected Noah to follow those instructions with excellence. Providing a detailed set of instructions created the expectation that Noah would follow through—yes, with hard work, but also with excellent work.

Effort is not the same as excellence. Read that sentence again, because we often assume that effort and excellence are one and the same when it comes to glorifying God. But they're not. Both are important and needed, and when combined, they produce a glorifying product.

Athlete, are you becoming excellent at your craft? Are you putting in the necessary preparation and practice time to maximize your abilities? God desires that you give your best effort, but he also wants you to maximize the skill set he gave you to steward.

Error #4: You Shouldn't Pray for Success

It should come as no surprise that prayer brings glory to God (Phil. 4:19; Acts 10:4; Eph. 1:14). He is exalted as worthy when we show our dependence on him. When we thank God for the opportunity to play or for some success we've enjoyed, we are saying, "What I just experienced was a gift, and I want to recognize you as the giver of that gift."

I once asked a large group of Division I athletes if it was okay for athletes to pray that God would help them win or succeed. Every athlete predictably shook his or her head no. Regardless of whether or not the athletes had actually done it, there seemed to be this belief that it was wrong to ask for such a thing. Here's the truth: every athlete wants permission to pray for a win, or at least for a personal best performance.

And I'm ready to give that permission to you. Yes, go ahead and pray for the win. Pray for your success.

Are there better things to pray for besides winning and success? Sure. Nevertheless, when we ask God in prayer to help us win or play well, we give him glory. Think about it. When you pray, you are acknowledging that you can't do it on your own. You are admitting that you need God's help. When we pray to God for or about anything, we are showing our dependence on him and bringing him glory in the process. We show that we are sheep who lack the ability to get what we want without our shepherd to help.

Jesus says in John 15:5, "I am the vine; you are the branches. Whoever abides in me and I in him, he it is that bears much fruit, for apart from me you can do nothing."

Apart from me, you can do nothing.

When my kids were young, they struggled tying their shoes. I got glory not when they sat in the corner and tried to do it themselves but when they carried their footwear over to me, asked for help, and then patiently sat while I put their shoes on for them. I also got glory when they looked up afterward and said, "Thanks, Daddy!"

Similarly, we glorify God when the prayers we offer up about our sport include thankfulness, praise, and asking.

In a culture that reveres athletes as gods, prayer becomes a simple way for us to confess this: "You are God, I am not, and I need your help. Thank you." If you want to pray for athletic success, go for it.

Keep in mind that God wants you to come to him as you are, not how you think you should be. In other words, he wants honest prayers. At the same time, in coming as you are, you may discover that he changes your desires over time. Herbert McCabe, a priest and theologian, once explained how this works:

> When you pray, consider what you want and need and never mind how vulgar or childish it might appear. If you want very much to pass that exam or get to know that girl or boy better, that is what you should pray for. You could let world peace rest for a while. You may not be ready yet to want that passionately. When you pray you must come before God as

honestly as you can. There is no point in pretending
to *him*. One of the great human values of prayer is
that you face the facts about yourself and admit to
what you want; and you know you can talk about
this to God because he is totally loving and accept-
ing. In true prayer you must meet God and meet
yourself where you really are, for it is just by this that
God will move you on from where you really are. For
prayer is a bit of a risk. If you pray and acknowledge
your most infantile desires, there is every danger that
you may grow up a bit, that God will grow you up.
When (as honestly as you can) you speak to God of
your desires, very gently and tactfully he will often
reveal to you that in fact you have deeper and more
mature desires. But there is only one way to find this
out: to start from where you are. It is no good pretending to yourself that you are full of high-minded
aspirations. You have to wait until you are.[3]

Now that we have addressed some of the lies about how
Christian athletes think about winning, it's time to focus on some
positive ways to deal with winning and success that glorify God.

Use the Gifts God Has Given You to Play Your Best and Try to Win

The end goal of a competition is for someone to come out on top.
That's why you play the game. There's nothing sinful or evil about
that.

First Corinthians 9:24 says, "Do you not know that in a race all the runners run, but only one receives the prize? So run that you may obtain it." Now, I realize that Paul is using sports as a metaphor for the Christian life here, but the foundation of the metaphor is that sports have a winner and a loser.

Should a Christian athlete want to win? Yes, that is the point of the game. Does God want a Christian athlete to have a desire to win? Yes, that is the right desire. I would hope that God puts a desire in the heart of a contractor to see a finely built house. I would hope that God puts a desire in the heart of an accountant to see well-prepared, accurate financial statements. I would hope that God puts a desire in the heart of a doctor to correctly diagnose a patient.

While there's a sense in which sports are just a game, that doesn't mean they don't matter or that your efforts and desires related to them don't matter. They most certainly do! God made you with your athletic gifts and gave you a desire for competition for a reason. So try your best to win.

Enjoy the Win; Then Move toward Him

Pastor Matt Chandler has used the "Grand Canyon example" in a few of his sermons to make a similar point. It goes like this: Imagine seeing the Grand Canyon for the first time. Your immediate thought might be, *This is incredible!* That's a natural response. An unnatural response would be stepping to the edge of the Grand Canyon and saying, "*I* am incredible."

Seeing something amazing should create a sense of awe that points outside of yourself. After all, you were created to enjoy good gifts and the emotions that spring forth when you experience them.

Christians have the ability to take these types of experiences and deepen their joy even more.

As a Christian, seeing the Grand Canyon and all its majesty is an opportunity for you to take your thoughts one step further by attributing the creation or experience to God and his goodness: "God, you are incredible for creating this! Thank you!"

> The giver of any gift is glorified when the recipient experiences joy and recognizes the giver with thanks.

The beauty and majesty of the Grand Canyon triggers worship in a believer. The awe-filled experience leads the Christian to praise God for the awesomeness of his creation. Like my experience with the hole in one, having someone to celebrate it with you completes the experience. When we celebrate with God, we not only complete an experience, but we maximize it. It might sound a little like this: "Wow! That is amazing! Thank you, God, for creating it! You are amazing! Thank you for giving me the opportunity to experience this with you!"

The giver of any gift is glorified when the recipient experiences joy and recognizes the giver with thanks.

So, athlete, it's good to care about winning, and it's good to win. Enjoy your wins and successes. But share those experiences with God. Thank him for the temporary happiness that winning creates. Thank him for the memories you make with teammates and others. In thanking him, acknowledge that he alone can give you ultimate satisfaction.

Humbly Accept Praise

If you win and a reporter or a fan congratulates you, what are you supposed to do? Let's not overcomplicate this. It's not prideful to say "thank you" for the compliment. It's polite. A win or success is not always going to get you in front of reporters begging for a great quote. What a win does afford you, however, is an opportunity to practice humility and show that while the win was great, God is better still.

In his book *Practicing Affirmation*, Sam Crabtree tells about Corrie ten Boom, who had a unique strategy for graciously handling praise.

> When people would honor her, she knew that God was really the one who deserved all the glory and credit, so she would imagine each honor as a huge bouquet of roses. She would picture herself taking in their scent and savoring it for a moment before handing it up to him, the rightful recipient. Smell the roses and hand them up.[4]

What are some ways you can celebrate wins with class and humility? One simple way is to shake your opponent's hand after the competition. That's a good application of Philippians 2:4, which says, "Let each of you look not only to his own interests, but also to the interests of others." You should also thank the referees for their service, even if you didn't agree with every call. It's also a good practice to encourage your teammates with what they did well during the competition, win or lose.

If you did something in the competition that you regret, you should apologize to the person you offended, whether opponent, official, coach, or teammate. Romans 12:18 says, "If possible, so far as it depends on you, live peaceably with all." There's no need to make enemies before, during, or after the game. Winning doesn't erase any ungodliness that happened during the competition. It's your responsibility as a Christ-follower to take ownership for your part and to seek reconciliation. That's what humility is all about. And it is glorifying to God.

Questions for Individual Reflection or Team Study

What has been the biggest highlight of your career up to this point? What made it so special?

Of the four errors in perspective the author described, which one stood out to you the most? Why?

What do you think of the statement "celebration completes the highs we experience in sports"?

How do you think you can balance the fact that sport offers such great moments of happiness with the fact that it will never ultimately satisfy the true desire of our hearts?

Describe the difference between effort and excellence. Why are both essential in our attempt to glorify God through sports?

Why does the author think it's okay to pray for a win or success in sports?

Additional Questions for Coaches to Consider

After reading this chapter and thinking about the culture you have helped create with your athlete(s), are there any adjustments you need to make? What are they?

How do you teach athletes to pursue winning but still maintain perspective?

How would you describe your philosophy or theology of winning to other coaches?

How could having a theology of winning assist you in glorifying God?

5

On Losing

Faithless is he that says farewell when the road darkens.

J. R. R. Tolkien (Gimli), *The Fellowship of the Ring*

No competitive athlete enjoys losing, Christian or not. With the amount of time and energy we put into training and preparing, any nonwinning outcome is sure to bring frustration. But we would be wrong to think a losing effort can't bring glory to God.

As in the chapter on winning, we first need to address some of the poor thinking surrounding the topic of losing before we get into practical advice on how to steward a losing outcome for the glory of God.

Error #1: Don't Be Frustrated When You Lose

The Bible study had gotten away from me. When you lead a Bible study, you need wisdom and discernment to decide when to stay on track and when to follow rabbit trails. At this point, we were not on track. We had even veered away from the rabbit trail.

Though this Bible study with the cross-country guys was supposedly about the rich man and Lazarus from Luke 16, I now found myself listening to a monologue about what it looks like to respond in a godly way when we fail. My mind must have wandered for a few minutes, during which time this runner had seized control of the study.

"Take last week," the junior on the team explained. "I was racing the 5k in Iowa and had to drop out. Was I upset? Sure. But I knew it wasn't right to show that frustration outwardly because everyone was watching. Even God. What kind of Christian would I have been if I would have looked overly upset?"

We can correct this lie with the Bible, but we can also use some common sense. If the natural emotion that comes from winning is happiness culminating in celebration, it only makes sense that the natural emotions that follow a loss are frustration and disappointment. But Christian culture tells us to bottle up those reactions. It's important to know, then, that when things go wrong, it is okay to feel frustrated and disappointed. You're human, after all.

The problem is when your disappointment causes you to sin. Ephesians 4:26 gives us a great life principle that we can use in response to a loss or disappointment in the context of sports: "Be angry and do not sin; do not let the sun go down on your anger." The sin is not in the disappointment we feel, but where the disappointment could potentially lead us.

This verse also teaches us to try to limit our frustration (anger) to a particular period of time and not let it go on indefinitely. Specifically, it says we should not go to bed angry. The context of the verse relates to interpersonal relationships, but hanging on to anger about anything will, at the very least, interrupt your sleep, and at worst, lead to bitterness and a whole host of other sins.

What are some of these sins? In his book *Game Day for the Glory of God*, Stephen Altrogge names three temptations following a loss:

we can be quick to criticize others, we can agonize over the defeat, or we can succumb to feelings of shame.[1] I would add to the list that we can become short with our coaches, teammates, opponents, and fans. Basically, we can become irritable, self-absorbed, and discouraged. Athlete, you have permission to be upset personally, but just be careful it does not cause you to lash out relationally.

Error #2: You Have Less of an Impact for God When You Lose

After God brought his people out of slavery in Egypt and onto the path to the Promised Land, he gave Moses a set of laws for the people to follow. In addition to aligning themselves with the character and purposes of God, these laws also set the Israelites apart from other nations. We see it explained in Deuteronomy this way:

> See, I have taught you statutes and rules, as the LORD my God commanded me, that you should do them in the land that you are entering to take possession of it. Keep them and do them, for that will be your wisdom and your understanding in the sight of the peoples, who, when they hear all these statutes, will say, "Surely this great nation is a wise and understanding people." (Deut. 4:5–6)

God gave them laws and told them how to act so they would stand out from the surrounding nations. The idea was that other nations would take notice and say, "Wow! Look how different they are from everyone else." And then those nations would ask, "What is it about them that causes them to act the way they do?" The Israelites were meant to be a peculiar people, a light to the nations. (Of course, they ultimately failed in their calling, and Christ accomplished what they couldn't.)

I'm not making a direct comparison between today's athlete and the Israelites. But there is a principle here to understand. When God's people look different from the rest of society, society tends to notice. This theme is seen in the New Testament and throughout the history of the church. God's people are called to practice obedience throughout trying circumstances. When they do, people take heed. Culture changes. Movements of justice and human flourishing rise up.

When a Christian athlete is victorious, people expect him or her to give credit to God. What culture doesn't expect is for someone to acknowledge God even when that person loses. Athlete, your struggles on the playing field do not minimize your platform for Christ. In fact, your platform may be even greater following a loss. A loss can be an opportunity to shatter the cultural expectation.

 We would be wrong to think a losing effort can't bring glory to God.

Something I've observed from working in sports ministry is that when Christian athletes win and use their platform to talk about Jesus, Christians notice and want to hear more from that athlete. When Christian athletes lose and still make much of Jesus, it's non-Christians who notice and want to hear more from that athlete.

Anyone can talk about how awesome Jesus is on the heels of a win or outstanding performance. Our culture's idea of happiness is attached to the blessings we experience in life. That's why losing affords us an opportunity to show that our joy in Christ transcends outward circumstances. So stand out from the crowd when you've experienced a tough loss. Feel the freedom to be a Christian athlete and be disappointed at the outcome of a competition, but rebound quickly and don't let any residual negative emotions lead you to being a jerk.

Simply maintaining perspective can be a powerful witness. Athletic success may build the platform that brings you attention, but how you respond to a loss might be what allows you to capitalize on it for the glory of God.

Here are a few ways you can look different to a watching world when you lose:

- Thank God for the opportunity to compete.
- Lead both teams in prayer after the competition.
- Shake your opponent's hand.
- Affirm your teammates with encouraging words.
- Thank the referees or officials.
- Honor your coaches by respectfully listening to what they have to say.
- Leverage social media in a genuine way that shows you have perspective on the loss.

Athlete, God is glorified when our obedience to him causes us to look different from everyone else. Don't waste your losses.

Error #3: If You Are Disobedient in Your Personal Life, God Is Less Likely to Bless You with a Win

If you lost, it's not because you neglected to pray hard enough, or sinned earlier in the week, or didn't have enough faith. To believe that would mean you would have won if you had done the right things. God cannot be manipulated that way.

I once talked with an athlete who was convinced God had promised him success. The promises were specific: NCAA championship. MVP. First pick overall. Even the team that would eventually draft him. When none of those came true, he had to choose one of three reasons:

1. He had heard incorrectly.
2. God had lied to him.
3. He didn't have enough faith.

He chose number three. He opted to believe that God did have great things in store for him—but only if he held up his end of the bargain. He needed to be obedient in all situations or God would take back his promises. He needed to believe with all his heart, leaving no room for a sliver of doubt, or God would withhold those promises. He didn't see it, but he was trying to manipulate God into getting what he wanted.

We've all done it before. Some of us may still do it. We have used God like a four-leaf clover or another good luck charm for our personal gain, win, or power. We understand we don't deserve free gifts, so we try to behave better. We work as hard as we can to refrain from sin in the days and hours leading to competition, and then we pray that God will bless us for being so righteous. In fact, we're pretty sure God owes us. It would be funny if it weren't true.

 If you lost, it's not because you neglected to pray hard enough, or sinned earlier in the week, or didn't have enough faith.

The beauty of the gospel is that God does not bless us based on our awesomeness, but on his. Second Corinthians 5:21 says, "For our sake he made him to be sin who knew no sin, so that in him we might become the righteousness of God." We don't need to perform for God in order for him to bless us. Jesus already accomplished everything that his Father wanted on our behalf.

For many of us, the danger isn't in trusting him for big things he never promised in the first place but in thinking he will reward obedience with athletic success and withhold it when we are disobedient. That's not a belief in the biblical God—that's a belief in karma.

Our obedience should arise from a desire to please our heavenly Father, not out of a misguided belief that our goodness can be exchanged for an earthly blessing like athletic success. God is not a genie or a lucky rabbit's foot. He is King, Savior, and Father. Ask what you want of him on the basis of who he is, not who you are.

How can we handle losing better and respond to a loss in a way that glorifies God? Three things come to mind.

Confess

Can we be honest here? Most Christian athletes will respond to a loss in a sinful way, whether through outward actions or just in our thoughts. Sometimes the simplest way to glorify God is through confessing your sin to him. Here's a prayer I have prayed many times:

> God, please forgive me for my actions following the loss today. I placed more value on the outcome of a game than I did on my allegiance to you. Forgive me for being so fixated on winning that it led me to sin. I need your grace to move forward. Help me find contentment in you, not in the outcome of a game. And give me the grace to do better next time. Amen.

Gain Perspective

Maintaining perspective is key. Here's some mic-dropping truth from Stephen Altrogge:

> No matter how significant they may seem, all our wins and losses are very insignificant in the grand scheme of things. There are no lives hanging in the balance, nor is the peace of the free world dependent on whether we win or lose. God's kingdom will continue to advance even if our softball team doesn't.[2]

At the end of the day, it's a game you're playing. Your internal and external responses should reflect that reality. As we've said, it's understandable that you'd be upset in the moments after a loss. However, a Christian athlete's mourning period following a loss should be pretty short. Real tragedy comes not when we lose the game but when we lose focus on what God prioritizes: our heart's response to adversity.

If we want to have a proper perspective on losing and respond in a way that pleases God and brings us contentment, we need to pay attention to what's going on in our hearts following a loss. Here are some good questions to ask yourself after a losing effort (and yes, I realize that nobody wants to go through reflection questions after they just lost):

- Do I have sinful anger in my heart over the loss, or am I simply a little frustrated that I put in so much hard work and fell short this time?
- Are what-if questions consuming my thought life?
- Am I thinking poorly of my teammates or coaches because of what happened?
- Am I acting like Jesus would toward my teammates, opponents, coaches, and refs following the game?

Look for the Wins

I grew up playing every sport imaginable. For someone who would eventually run track and cross-country, I was actually a pretty coordinated athlete. (If you have ever seen a runner try to play a sport that involves a ball, you know what I'm talking about.)

But coordination means very little when you enter high school at four feet ten inches and ninety-five pounds. My small stature— and the fact that I was just not as good as I thought I was—caused me to not make the team in three sports my first three weeks as a freshman. I was devastated. But God had a bigger win in mind. My youth pastor tells the story better than I could:

> Josh burst into my office with a freshman guy named Brian. It seems Brian had been cut from the team. For the third time. Three sports in a row— *whack, whack, whack.* That had to be a record at our school. Most kids sank into depression after one cut. But three?
>
> So there they stood in front of me. Before I could say anything, Josh got in my face and announced, "Me and Brian are starting our own basketball league and we need the church gym. You got a problem with that?"...
>
> Now a decade later, Josh has a good job, a wonderful wife, and kids of his own. And this year he's helping oversee the basketball league he and Brian started. You see, their league not only survived—it's become a legend in our area. In its tenth season at this writing, the Blythefield Basketball Association (BBA) is student-led, supports 280 players on 28 teams, and features a website, employees, refs, draft day, trades, a full set of stats, and cell-phone-toting

agents. What's more, students share the gospel over one hundred times each year during halftime at these games. As a result, thousands have been introduced to Christ, many join small groups, and sometimes entire families land in church.[3]

Let me give you another example of how God has used a loss to give me something better than a win ever could. Eventually, I ended up on the cross-country team—mainly because it was one of the only sports you can't get cut from. After working hard for three years, things started to click for me, and my race times dropped significantly. The fall of my junior year, our team was one of the top-ranked cross-country programs in the entire United States. We were good. Really good. Winning the state meet should have been a formality, but something happened.

With a mile to go, my body stopped working, and I collapsed into a crowd of screaming fans. Ten minutes later, I found myself in a medical tent with IVs in both arms and my parents by my side. My coach stopped by to check on me—or to just tell me the news. We had lost. I had cost my team the state title. I was devastated.

As I sat on that cot, one of the girls on the team popped her head in the tent and asked if I was okay. She asked if she could pray for me. And she did. We had never really talked up to this point, partly because of the size of our cross-country program but mostly because she was way out of my league. But Linsey Blaisdell was drawn to people in need. And this was about as needy as I could get.

Her name is now Linsey Smith, and we have three kids.

We started dating a few months after my dreadful state meet performance, and we have literally been together ever since—all because I lost the state meet for our team. At the time, I would have given anything to stand on that podium. Knowing how God blessed my life through that loss, however, I would gladly lose a thousand times over. God used the biggest loss of my life to give me what has been my greatest blessing.

Often, losing feels like a step back, a missed opportunity. It's hard to see how anything good could come from a loss. We would do well to remember that God often works in ways that are different from what we would expect. Isaiah 55:8 reminds us that our thoughts fail to align with his thoughts and our ways of doing things are different than his.

In light of that truth, we need to ask this question: What opportunities does losing provide? This requires that we pay attention to what is going on around us after a losing effort. Even if the door to winning slammed shut, what other doors could God be opening?

Remember, your sport is a vehicle to help you love and serve God and others. It's not just for you. We can't make a deal with God that our obedience must be rewarded with wins.

God has shown that his blueprint for expanding his kingdom often involves seemingly backward methods. He asked Abraham to sacrifice his own son, a son through whom God had said he would bless all nations. He asked Gideon to drastically reduce the number of men in his army before going to battle. He told Joshua to march his army around Jericho for a week blowing trumpets instead of attacking the walls. He took everything from Job instead of rewarding him for his obedience. He sent his one and only Son to die in our place.

Get the point? Just because things didn't work out the way you wanted or expected doesn't mean God isn't up to something good. Ask him what he is doing, and express an openness to join him in it.

A word of caution before moving on. By his grace, God allowed me to see the good that came out of a couple of horrible losses in my life. One took a year to see; the other took about six years. I've had other losses about which I still wonder what God is or was doing in allowing them. The point is that we are not entitled to know. Maybe God will show us, and maybe he won't. But I have to believe he wants us to trust that he is up to something good, even when the scoreboard doesn't fall in our favor.

Get Better

You never know what's in a sponge until you squeeze it. You can make some assumptions about what's inside, but until you compress it, you won't really know. God can use our losses as a sponge to bring some of the nastiness inside us out into the light. And that is a loving thing for him to do. For us to be molded into the likeness of Jesus, we need to know what needs molding.

James 1:2–4 takes it to another level when it says, "Count it all joy, my brothers, when you meet trials of various kinds, for you know that the testing of your faith produces steadfastness. And let steadfastness have its full effect, that you may be perfect and complete, lacking in nothing."

What comes out of you when you're "squeezed" by defeat? What do you notice about your attitude or your actions after a loss? Do they reveal entitlement? Anger? Bitterness? A complaining spirit? A tendency to shift blame? Losing gives you an opportunity to look in the mirror at your response and see where you need to change. While losing a competition amounts to an earthly loss, it can help you win huge spiritual gains.

> Just because things didn't work out the way you wanted or expected doesn't mean God isn't up to something good.

Athlete, don't waste your losses. Use them to grow. Continue to put your hope in God. Trust him with the unknown. Show by your attitude that he is enough, and confess where you have fallen short. Commit to changing the revealed weaknesses he shows you. And finally, take the wise advice of Dr. Seuss (which conveniently aligns with the biblical truth of Philippians 3:12–16): "When something bad happens you have three choices. You can either let it define you, let it destroy you, or you can let it strengthen you."[4]

Questions for Individual Reflection or Team Study

What has been the lowlight of your career up to this point? What made it so hard?

Which of the three errors most resonates with you?

How do you think we should balance the tension of wanting to make God look great with not coming across as indifferent after a loss? How can we allow ourselves the freedom to be upset but also have the awareness that we can influence others by the way we respond to adversity?

Think back to some losses or adversity you have faced in your career. Is there any good that came from those experiences?

What's your response to the statement "Your sport is a vehicle to help you love and serve God and others"?

Additional Questions for Coaches to Consider

Describe what happens both internally and externally in the moments after a loss.

How you behave after a loss often reveals what you value most. How do you think your athletes, staff, and family experience you after a loss?

How long does it typically take you to look past the loss and look forward to what's next?

How do you wrestle with the reality that God can be glorified through a loss *and* that your job may be dependent on your program winning?

6

On Injuries

The most painful times in our lives are times in which …
our idols are being threatened or removed.

Tim Keller, *Counterfeit Gods*

When I understand that everything happening
to me is to make me more Christlike, it
resolves a great deal of anxiety.

A. W. Tozer

Injuries are awful. Anybody who has played sports has had to deal with them to some extent. (If you haven't, count your blessings, but know that injuries are usually part of the deal.) While physical pain is associated with injuries, there are other, greater factors that contribute to their awfulness.

Injuries prevent us from playing at 100 percent and rob us of the optimal level of performance we work so hard to reach. Injuries can halt any momentum we may have gained in our training. They can sideline us not only from competition but also from our community, as we now spend our practice time on the training table instead of with teammates. Injuries can even leave us uncertain about our future in the sport.

Will I get better? If I do recover, will I return to peak form or merely be a hobbled version of my former self? Will I be able to play without fear, or will I always be a little cautious? When I return, will I still have my spot, or will a teammate have stepped in and grabbed it?

Despite the validity of questions like these, for the Christian athlete the biggest question tends to be this: *Why would God allow something like this to happen?* As we have done with other topics, we want to look at how we can use an injury (and the circumstances surrounding the injury) to deepen our relationship with God and glorify him through it.

It starts with being honest with him.

I remember sitting down with a guy I was discipling who played defensive tackle for a D1 football team. He was a senior. It was early in the college football season, and his name was already showing up in mock drafts on the internet. He was going to live out his dream of playing in the NFL, as long as he stayed healthy. As he was chasing down an opposing player, his knee twisted, and he fell to the ground. He tore his MCL. His future was now uncertain, yet when I met with him, he tried to stay positive.

"I know God's got me," he said.

"Are you frustrated? Have you told him how you feel? He can handle it, you know. Be honest with him," I pressed, "Don't treat him like the media and give rehearsed lines that sound good but don't reflect how you feel." I could see tears starting to well up in his eyes.

He came back the next week a changed man. His MCL didn't miraculously heal. He still faced a lot of uncertainty. But he had been honest with God about his frustrations and felt the freedom to cry out to him in anger and disappointment. In doing so, he began a process that every Christian athlete needs to wrestle with if he or she wants to leverage an injury to glorify God.

Dr. Henry Cloud points out in his book *Changes That Heal*, "Real intimacy always comes in the company of truth."[1] Relationships are healthy and grow when honesty is present. God can handle our honesty. He has a big enough chest for us to pound on it from time to time.

He Can Handle It

King David in the Bible models well for us what it looks like to come before God without polished religious phrases. He approached God in prayer with a rawness that I envy. Here are a few examples from the book of Psalms where David cried out to the Lord with brutal honesty:

- I cried aloud (3:4).
- I was in distress (4:1).
- Consider my groaning (5:1).
- I am languishing (6:2).
- My bones are troubled (6:2).
- My soul also is greatly troubled (6:3).
- I am weary with my moaning (6:6).
- I flood my bed with tears (6:6).
- See my affliction (9:13).

- How long must I … have sorrow in my heart all
  the day? (13:2).
- I find no rest (22:2).
- I am lonely and afflicted (25:16).
- The troubles of my heart are enlarged (25:17).

The prophet Jeremiah cried out to God, "O LORD, you have deceived me, and I was deceived; you are stronger than I, and you have prevailed. I have become a laughingstock all the day; everyone mocks me" (Jer. 20:7). That is bold. But God can handle it.

Perhaps we have no greater example of what it looks like to come before God with raw honesty than Jesus himself. Before he was betrayed by Judas and went to the cross, he prayed the same prayer three times to the Father: "My Father, if it be possible, let this cup pass from me; nevertheless, not as I will, but as you will" (Matt. 26:39). Jesus knew the plan, was anxious about it, and was honest before God about how he was feeling in that moment.

God Already Knows Anyway

The second reason we should be honest with God is that he already knows what we are feeling. Listen again to Jeremiah: "O LORD of hosts, who tests the righteous, who sees the heart and the mind, let me see your vengeance upon them, for to you have I committed my cause" (Jer. 20:12). Jeremiah plainly says that God sees the mind and the heart. He knows what we are thinking.

On multiple occasions, Jesus also perceived the thoughts of those around him (Matt. 9:4; 22:18; Mark 2:8; Luke 6:8; 11:17).

Have you ever played hide-and-seek with a little kid? If so, you know kids are awful at the game. They usually hide in the same place you hid when it was your turn, and when they try someplace new, they often end up curled in a ball under a blanket in the middle of the room with their eyes closed.

Trying to hide our real emotions from God is like playing hide-and-seek with him. We are the unimaginative kids who hide in plain sight. It's a futile game to engage in with an all-knowing God. Be honest with God about what you are feeling when you are injured. He already knows how you feel, and he can handle it. And it will help you deal with the injury when you include him in the process.

Gain Perspective

After we get honest with God, we need to gain some perspective. Perspective on injuries is a little like Advil—it's not going to heal us, but it makes the pain a bit more manageable.

Having perspective opens the door for us to hope. When we know God has a plan, even if we are not thrilled about it, we realize that God is telling a bigger story than our current circumstances allow us to see. Why would God allow you to get injured? Here are a few possible reasons:

- He is preparing you for something in the future.
- He wants you to deal with something in the present.
- He wants to use you to reach someone.
- He is strengthening your faith.

He Is Preparing You for Something in the Future

Perhaps God is using the circumstance of your injury to prepare you for something in the future.[2] The Bible has no shortage of examples of God's people going through seemingly insignificant circumstances only to later discover that those very circumstances played a vital role in shaping their readiness for future opportunities.

Joseph exemplifies a man who refused to be defined by his circumstances. His brothers sold him into slavery because they were jealous of him, and then Potiphar threw him into prison on a false accusation of attempted rape. He could have easily lived in bitterness and self-pity. Instead, he chose to remain faithful to the Lord. While in prison, Joseph interpreted the dreams of two fellow inmates and then later of Pharaoh's. Pharaoh was impressed. He elevated Joseph to second-in-command of all of Egypt. Joseph leveraged his new position of authority to prepare the nation of Egypt—and his family—for the coming famine. His position and wisdom in preparation saved everyone.

Let's look at David. When Samuel came to Jesse's house to find the next king of Israel, Jesse brought out his sons for examination. There was only one problem: he forgot David. Often overlooked as the youngest of the brothers, David spent years riding the bench. While his brothers were off at battle, David was shepherding the family's sheep and working on his slingshot skills. But when Goliath challenged any man in Israel to a one-on-one battle, David was ready. With one accurately placed shot, he took down Goliath and claimed victory for God's people.

Tamar's husband died. Her dead husband's brother was supposed to marry her, but he died too. Judah, her father-in-law, promised to give her his third son. He didn't. We later read that Judah saw a woman on the side of the road, thought she was a prostitute, and slept with her. The woman turned out to be—you guessed it—Tamar. She had twins as a result of this inappropriate one-day stand. One of the boys was named Perez. We read in Matthew's genealogy that Jesus Christ came from the lineage of Perez.

Athlete, you never know what God could have in store for your future. Trust that he sees you in your present circumstances. Trust that he is in control. And trust that he is good.

He Wants You to Deal with Something in the Present

Pastor Matt Chandler once said:

> God is not the ambulance driver that shows up after the wreck. He's the surgeon that will make the cut, knowing exactly what to cut out, exactly what to leave in, exactly what to take, exactly what to let alone. This is the giant, scary, worthy-of-worship, eternal God of the Bible, who not only knows tomorrow but is already there.[3]

This is a scary truth to wrestle with. God loves us so much that sometimes he acts as a surgeon and proactively removes the problem before it causes us greater harm. Perhaps your injury is God putting you on the sideline because something is going on inside you that you refuse to address. Maybe, in his love, he is taking away the distraction of your sport to force you to deal with it. It wouldn't be the first time God has done something like that.

Jonah was an interesting guy. We know he was a prophet, called to be God's mouthpiece. His job was pretty simple: hear a message from God and share it with the people. But God knew there was some pruning that needed to happen in Jonah's heart, so he gave Jonah an assignment: tell the people of Nineveh to repent. Jonah tried to run away and not deal with the issue, so God stepped in and instructed a large fish to swallow Jonah after he was thrown out of a boat. Jonah repented, went to Nineveh, and shared God's message with the people. The entire city of Nineveh repented, and God spared them—and Jonah was furious. He didn't want God to save those "evil" people. God knew there was pride growing in the heart of Jonah, so he forced Jonah to confront it.

Sometimes we are so distracted by what is happening with our sport that we are unaware of the dangerous trajectory our hearts are on. God may be using an injury to force you to deal with an issue in your life that you are currently ignoring because you are so pre-occupied with your athletic career.

He Wants to Use You to Reach Someone

Second Corinthians 5:17–20 shines a light on an incredible truth:

> If anyone is in Christ, he is a new creation. The old
> has passed away; behold, the new has come. All this
> is from God, who through Christ reconciled us to
> himself and gave us the ministry of reconciliation;
> that is, in Christ God was reconciling the world to
> himself, not counting their trespasses against them,
> and entrusting to us the message of reconciliation.

Therefore, we are ambassadors for Christ, God making his appeal through us. We implore you on behalf of Christ, be reconciled to God.

Translation: Once you become a Christian, you become a missionary.

Whether you consider yourself a missionary or not doesn't matter. *God* considers you one, and his opinion will always trump yours. We have been given the "ministry of reconciliation" and are "ambassadors for Christ." We have a north star now, a life's purpose.

> Your responsibility as a Christian who happens to be an athlete is to consistently ask yourself this question: *Who might God want me to reach where I am right now?*

While a sport may be an important pursuit for a Christian, it is not his or her primary objective. Our primary objective as Christians is to love God and love others (Matt. 22:36–39). An overflow of this purpose becomes sharing God's message of love, grace, and forgiveness with the people around us.

Your responsibility as a Christian who happens to be an athlete is to consistently ask yourself this question: *Who might God want me to reach where I am right now?*

Injuries force you to stop your normal rhythms. Your schedule looks different. The places where you spend your time are different. And the people you spend time with are different. Doctors. Nurses.

Trainers. Injured teammates. Injured athletes who are not a part of your team. The new network of people you spend time with becomes the new scope of your mission field.

Athlete, God may have allowed you to be injured at this particular moment because it forces you to spend time with someone who desperately needs to hear about the love he freely offers through Christ. And God has granted you the privilege to be the one who tells this person. It certainly would not be the first time God has used tough circumstances as a means to relocate his people for the advancement of the gospel.

In Acts 16:22–34, Paul and Silas were stripped down, severely beaten, and thrown in jail. That same night, a violent earthquake shook the prison and loosened the chains of the prisoners. Paul and Silas were free. But they didn't flee. They knew they were not in that prison by accident. There was a purpose in their present pain. They ended up sharing the good news of Jesus with the jailer, and he was saved that very night.

The possible ripple effects of his conversion are fun to imagine. As Christians around the city would continue to be persecuted and thrown into jail, this jailer may have been the person who watched over them, cared for them, and encouraged them. Only the Lord knows the good that flowed out of this man's life because of the awareness and faithfulness of Paul and Silas to seize the opportunity to share their faith.

Maybe you are injured for a similar reason. That doctor, nurse, trainer, or student-trainer is in a unique position to serve and care for athletes. What if that medical professional's future care consisted not only of meeting physical needs but spiritual needs as well? The ripple effects could be far greater than we can imagine.

He Is Strengthening Your Faith

An easy mistake to make (and I was guilty of this too) is believing that sports are the primary outlet for God's blessing on your life instead of the sharpening rod he uses to shape you into his likeness. What if God is using everything in your life as an athlete, including an injury, to draw you closer and reveal his character to you? What if he is using this to grow your faith?

Pastor and author Craig Groeschel says it like this:

> Peaks are nice, but you don't see many farms on mountaintops. Why? Because things grow better in valleys. Your time in the valley may not be pleasant, but it's in the valleys of life that you grow closer to God and stronger in your faith.[4]

There may not be an epic plan involved in the injury. But God uses all things to bring about his will, including his will for us to grow in Christlikeness. Often in the Bible, the pathway to growth and power is weakness. Paul even boasted about his weaknesses (2 Cor. 12:9–10).

Jesus will not waste those moments when you feel weak, stuck, and powerless. He is, after all, more concerned with your spiritual growth than your athletic goals. An injury doesn't have to be merely a physical setback. It can also be a spiritual springboard.

We Want to Be the Hero

There is one other thing worth mentioning, but it may be hard to hear: You are not entitled to know what the purpose of your injury is or what good will come from it.

It could be that the ripple effects of your injury are part of God's plan in ways that have no direct impact on you. Even so, you can be sure there is a purpose in everything and every situation. Perhaps your injury served the purpose of God doing something in the life of your teammate who took your spot.

Early on in the Old Testament, Moses gets a lot of press. Sure, he had his flaws—including being a stuttering, insecure murderer—but that didn't stop God from using him. What becomes easy to miss, however, is the fact that for four hundred years, the Israelites suffered at the hands of their slave masters. As my pastor likes to point out, "They made bricks and died." For four hundred years. These Israelites were a mere footnote in history.

> An easy mistake to make … is believing that sports are the primary outlet for God's blessing on your life instead of the sharpening rod he uses to shape you into his likeness.

As athletes, most of us want to be the hero at some level. Even when struggling through an injury, we want to be able to point to the reason and purpose behind it. We cry out to God, "Just tell me my role, and I will try to be as faithful as I can." Sometimes we are more like Moses, playing a central role in what's going on around us.

Other times, we play the role of the Israelites—seemingly forgotten, unimportant, a footnote in a bigger story.

Regardless of what is going on, know that your pain has a purpose. To be the best possible steward of your circumstances, including an injury, trust God and open your eyes and heart to his greater purposes rather than sit in self-pity. Be okay with the possibility that God may be up to something that has more to do with someone else than with you.

Your injuries will always be an opportunity to glorify God through trusting that he is in control and working all things together for your good—even if his idea of what's good doesn't initially align with yours.

Questions for Individual Reflection or Team Study

If you have experienced a significant injury, how did it affect your relationship with God?

Do you think God wants us to be brutally honest with him? Why or why not?

How can seeing God as a good Father positively impact the way you approach him when sidelined by an injury?

How can having a proper perspective on an injury make the process more manageable?

Of the four possible reasons God allows injuries, which resonates the most with you? Why?

Is anyone on your team injured? Would you consider praying for that person right now and then texting him or her some encouragement?

Additional Questions for Coaches to Consider

How do you typically deal with athletes when they are injured? Do you still give them adequate attention (love) or do you find yourself neglecting them until they are healthy again?

What do you think an injured athlete needs most from you as a coach?

Do you think it's part of your role to bring God into the conversation when your athlete gets injured? If so, what are some appropriate ways you could do that?

What are some practical ways coaches can show love to an injured athlete?

If you were an athlete, what was your experience with injuries?

7

On Practice

To have love as the guiding principle of our lives means that
our continual mindset in all we do should be "What will
serve the other person?" It is not "What will serve me?"

Matt Perman, *What's Best Next*

What is practice? Our culture thinks of it as just an opportunity to get better at something. But the Christian athlete's definition of *practice* must expand past the world's definition. A serious athlete will spend anywhere from twenty to forty hours a week at practice. That's a lot of time to devote to getting better at a sport. God has some other things going on while we are at practice that need our attention.

If there was ever a place within athletics where we need to apply some new, unfamiliar, and potentially uncomfortable concepts, it's practice. How does God want us to approach this important component of sport that Christians don't always view through a spiritual lens?

Practice Is about More Than You

At practice, who is doing the practicing? You are: You perform. You work. You repeat. You become proficient. *You. You. You.*

The very definition of practice assumes that you are the subject. No wonder it is so easy for us to get this one backward. In today's culture, practice is about you putting in the time and effort to get better.

For the Christian athlete, practice should also be about others, not yourself. It's an opportunity to show respect to your coaches by doing what they say, working hard, and showing humility. It's an opportunity to deepen relationships with your teammates.

Do a quick Google search for "selflessness and happiness." You'll find study after study concluding that having a mindset centered on others will lead you to experience the maximum amount of joy in life. Many of these studies claim to have unlocked a secret that has actually been hidden in plain sight. God has been telling us this from the beginning.

- Matthew 5:42: "Give to the one who begs from you, and do not refuse the one who would borrow from you."
- John 15:12–13: "This is my commandment, that you love one another as I have loved you. Greater love has no one than this, that someone lay down his life for his friends."
- Romans 15:1: "We who are strong have an obligation to bear with the failings of the weak, and not to please ourselves."
- Galatians 6:2: "Bear one another's burdens, and so fulfill the law of Christ."

- Philippians 2:3–4: "Do nothing from selfish ambition or conceit, but in humility count others more significant than yourselves. Let each of you look not only to his own interests, but also to the interests of others."
- Hebrews 6:10: "God is not unjust so as to overlook your work and the love that you have shown for his name in serving the saints, as you still do."
- Hebrews 13:16: "Do not neglect to do good and to share what you have, for such sacrifices are pleasing to God."

Is practice an opportunity to get better as an athlete? Absolutely. We glorify God when we give it our best (Col. 3:17). We must not neglect the desire to improve, but that motivation must be secondary. This sounds crazy, I know.

This is a major perspective shift, but it will take only a few adjustments to make.

Before you leave the locker room, make it a point to find a teammate and ask if he or she is ready to go. Doing so builds a habit into your workout—before it even begins—to think of someone else besides yourself.

After the workout, compliment one of your teammates for something that individual did well. When we see something commendable in others, whether in attitude or action, a Christ-honoring thing to do is point it out and praise it. Anything that even remotely mirrors one of Jesus' many excellencies is deserving of affirmation.

Simple enough? The real challenge will be incorporating this others-centered mindset during the workout itself. Again, this takes only a few minor habitual adjustments.

Remember the concept of having a focal point to serve as motivation? A focal point is something you can quickly concentrate on that realigns your focus to your ultimate motivation for playing your sport: glorifying God. You can—and should—have more than one focal point. Each one will serve as a different reminder.

Pick a practice focal point. The purpose of this visible reminder helps realign your focus from yourself to others during practice. When you see that focal point, ask yourself this simple question: "Who could use a word of encouragement right now?" It is a question, but it is also a prayer to God: "God, who needs you at this moment? How can I communicate your love through a simple word of encouragement?"

Christ calls his followers to put others first. And practice is a great opportunity to … practice this.

Practice Is about More Than Proficiency

The purpose of practice is to become proficient. Repeated actions lead us to the end goal of proficiency. And yet, for the Christian athlete, the purpose of practice transcends proficiency. For us, the purpose of practice is ultimately to glorify God.

 "Whatever you do, work heartily, as for the Lord and not for men." This verse covers it all for the athlete.

What does that mean? As we learned in chapter 1, we give glory to God as athletes when we think and act in a way that pleases him and draws attention to who he is. How do you do that in practice? One way is by simply practicing at a high level.

Colossians 3:23 says, "Whatever you do, work heartily, as for the Lord and not for men." This verse covers it all for the athlete. What kind of effort should you give? You should work hard. Who should you do it for? For the Lord. Who shouldn't you do it for? People, which is to say, your teammates, coaches, fans, and anyone else. And when should you do all this? Anytime you do anything in sports, practice included.

Your motivation in practice should be to engage in it as if you were doing it for the Lord. The Christian athlete should be the hardest-working athlete on earth because he or she is playing for an audience of One. What does this look like practically? Show up early. Stay late. Get in extra reps. Run an extra mile. Get in an extra lift session. Get additional treatment. By separating yourself from the pack with your work ethic, your teammates and coaches will get a small glimpse of the God you serve, an incredible by-product of playing for an audience of One.

As God's ambassador, you have been given the opportunity to represent God to your teammates and coaches. How hard you work, your energy level, and your attitude all reflect back on the God you serve. Practice becomes a key environment for influencing others for Jesus.

Competing like a beast will win you the respect of the outsiders watching you. But *practicing* like a beast will win you the respect of your teammates and coaches.

Practice Is about More Than Repetition

If you were to picture what practice looks like right now, you would most likely imagine yourself in action—performing, working, and repeating to get better. That's a big part of it, but we do ourselves a disservice when we limit practice to the field, track, pool, or court. When we relegate practice to the workout, we are in danger of missing out on one of the greatest blessings that comes with our sport: the relationships we form.

Practice is more than the actions we perform. Practice includes the drive, walk, or bike ride to the locker room. Practice includes the locker room banter among your teammates. Practice includes the cooldown and the stretching. Practice includes the ice baths and the treatment. Practice includes the shower and getting ready to go. And practice includes the drive, walk, or bike ride back to your dorm, house, or apartment. So it's not just the reps that matter; it's the whole process from beginning to end.

> Relationships will always have more lasting value and joy than the trophies we earn.

Why is it so important to widen our view of what practice is and when it takes place? It's vital for us to see how practice becomes one of the primary avenues that God gives us to build relationships. When we widen our parameters for what practice includes, we begin to see it as more than just preparation for the next competition.

Through competition, you will remember the performance.

Through practice, you will remember the people.

Relationships will always have more lasting value and joy than the trophies we earn. When we place a higher emphasis on the award, we are valuing the praise of people—represented by the trophy—over the friendship of people. That's a bad trade. Again, this is a major perspective shift that will take only a few minor adjustments. Here are some ways to have a more holistic view of practice:

- Don't travel alone. Go to and from the workout with a teammate.
- Don't zone out. Put the headphones down and engage with your teammates before and after the workout.
- Don't be an ambassador for Christ just during the workout. Be an ambassador in the locker room too. Ephesians 5:4 says, "Let there be no filthiness nor foolish talk nor crude joking, which are out of place, but instead let there be thanksgiving." Acting like that might make you stand out among your teammates, which is the point. And if you're consistent and don't come across as judgmental or holier-than-thou, they will usually respect how you conduct yourself.

Practice Is about More Than Work

Many athletes dread practice. To classify it as *work* is probably an understatement. Athletes endure practice because of the hope that it will produce long-term benefits. They see it as a necessary means to an end. The harder you work your muscles, the stronger they become. The joy comes from the competition—or rather the result of the competition—not the repetition experienced in practice.

At some level, every athlete will have a strained relationship with practice. But our faith can help us grow an appreciation for how God has designed the body to function. I am not talking about the ability of muscles to get stronger, which is reason enough to appreciate God's design, but something deeper that God offers to everyone. God has designed our bodies in such a way that when we exercise, we actually experience happiness.

How does this work? When you start working out, your brain interprets this as stress.[1] When your heart rate increases, your brain believes you are either fighting someone or fleeing from someone. As a way to protect yourself and your brain from this stress, your body releases a protein called BDNF (brain-derived neurotrophic factor).

If you ever wonder why you often feel at ease and have an added sense of clarity and happiness after working out, you can thank BDNF. It has both a protective and a reparative effect on your memory neurons, and it acts as a reset switch.

While your brain releases BDNF, it also releases endorphins, another chemical to fight stress. Researcher M. K. McGovern describes some of the benefits of endorphins: "These endorphins tend to minimize the discomfort of exercise and are even associated with a feeling of euphoria."[2]

Have you ever heard athletes refer to the feeling they get after running as a "runner's high"? Next time you hear that, be sure to correct them: "Actually, it's just your brain releasing BDNF."

I'm kidding. Don't do that.

Is practice tough? Absolutely. But now you can come to practice with an expectation that God is going to use physical exercise to increase your joy at that moment. You may be dreading going to practice today, but it could be the very thing that enables you to enjoy the rest of your day. God designed it that way and is glorified when the process works as he intended it. Seeing and experiencing practice from this new perspective could shift the trajectory of your daily grind from work—to worship.

It has been said, "There is no glory in practice, but without practice, there is no glory." It's true. For the athlete trying to gain human glory, practice is merely a means to an end. For the Christian athlete, however, practice serves a greater purpose. For the Christian athlete, practice is not about gaining glory at all; it's about giving glory.

Questions for Individual Reflection or Team Study

What does a typical day of practice look like for you?

Do you enjoy practice? Dread it? Endure it?

What is your biggest takeaway from this chapter?

Of the four perspective shifts the author lays out, which would be the easiest for you to start incorporating into your normal rhythms tomorrow? Which would be the hardest? Why?

What do we learn about God from how he wired the body to release BDNF and endorphins during exercise, giving us the ability to feel good in moments of discomfort?

If you were to begin viewing practice as an opportunity to serve others, what would be the biggest sacrifice you would have to make? Would it be worth it?

What are some practical ways you can start applying some of these shifts?

Additional Questions for Coaches to Consider

What is your philosophy on practice? What do you value? What do you reinforce? Is there anything you don't tolerate? If so, what?

What shaped your view of practice (from the previous question)?

What are some subtle, practical ways you could help your athletes shift their approach in practice to being others-centered instead of self-centered?

Besides being an opportunity to get better, what are some other perspectives you have on practice?

Imagine God sitting in on one of your practices—what do you think he would notice?

In light of the fact that God *is* present at every practice, are there any changes you need to make?

8

On Teammates

How you treat people reveals what you believe about God.

Jackie Hill Perry

Johnny was in a great spot. He was well liked and really skilled at whatever he did. Along with being outstanding, he had the additional benefit of knowing the position was guaranteed to be his. He was literally born to do this. You can imagine his shock when he found out it was given to someone else before he even had a chance to prove himself.

This has nothing to do with sports. Johnny was a biblical character referred to as Jonathan. His dad, Saul, was the king of Israel. As his son, Jonathan was the rightful heir to the throne. But don't imagine him as some stuck-up rich kid. Jonathan was very capable. He would have been a great king, but in the end, he wasn't given the opportunity.

King Saul started off as a great king but later disobeyed God's commands. So God went outside of Saul's family to choose the next king of Israel. He chose David. A short time later, David was invited by Saul (apparently Saul did not know David was next in line for the throne) to play the harp before him.

Soon after that, David killed Goliath. Two significant things happened after David's slingshot victory. One, he became great friends with Jonathan. Two, Saul became increasingly jealous of the attention David received from everyone in Israel.

These two realities—David's friendship with Jonathan and the jealousy toward him from King Saul—combined with the fact that David's future kingship would come at the expense of both of them, set the tension for the story. Saul's jealousy led him on a murderous rampage against David.

At that point, Jonathan had a choice: let David die and take his rightful spot on the throne after his dad's time was done, or go against his dad and help save the life of his friend—and his future king. He was in a no-win predicament.

Rather than complain, Jonathan chose to make the best of the situation. And because of his unselfish attitude, he became one of the greatest teammates this world has ever known. If we hit the film room to analyze his life, we would see ten things worth modeling in our own athletic context.

Great Teammates Have Ambition

> One day Jonathan the son of Saul said to the young man who carried his armor, "Come, let us go over to the Philistine garrison on the other side." But he did not tell his father. (1 Sam. 14:1)

Before David arrives on the scene, we catch a glimpse of the character and ambition of Jonathan. As the son of King Saul, Prince Jonathan had the right to the throne after his father's reign was over.

He didn't have to prove anything. The spot was his. We see that he wasn't satisfied with playing it safe, however. Without his father's knowledge—or permission—Jonathan set a plan in motion to conquer the Philistines.

 A certain level of humility is involved in knowing you can always learn something from someone else.

Great teammates are not passive. They have a personal ambition to be the best they can be. Even if they are the front-runners for the open spot on the team, they don't take it for granted.

Great Teammates Learn from Other Great Teammates

And his armor-bearer said to him, "Do all that is in your heart. Do as you wish. Behold, I am with you heart and soul." (14:7)

After Jonathan shared the plan, his armor-bearer, the only other person to go along with him, had his back. He put Jonathan's interests above his own. There is a huge difference between "I support you" and "I am with you heart and soul." They were going to succeed together or die together trying. His armor-bearer was a great teammate. As we will see later in the story, Jonathan took on a role similar to his armor-bearer's in his friendship with David.

Great teammates don't learn how to be great in isolation. They pay attention to those around them who are doing it well. A certain level of humility is involved in knowing you can always learn something from someone else.

Great Teammates Are Skillful

> Then Jonathan climbed up on his hands and feet, and his armor-bearer after him. And they fell before Jonathan, and his armor-bearer killed them after him. And that first strike, which Jonathan and his armor-bearer made, killed about twenty men within as it were half a furrow's length in an acre of land. (14:13–14)

Jonathan was a warrior. It can be easy to forget that since the book of 1 Samuel spends so much time talking about how he supported and loved David. Jonathan was not a junior varsity athlete vying for a varsity spot. The kid was all-state. He was great at what he did.

Why is this important? Because it's easy to assume that great teammates are just role-players. We figure they have to be great teammates because that's the role they fill on the team. But that's far from the truth. Being a great teammate isn't limited to the armor-bearers and the ones who ride the bench. We are all called to be great teammates, no matter what our role is on the team.

Great Teammates Take Responsibility for Their Actions

> Then Saul said to Jonathan, "Tell me what you have done." And Jonathan told him, "I tasted a

little honey with the tip of the staff that was in my
hand. Here I am; I will die." And Saul said, "God
do so to me and more also; you shall surely die,
Jonathan." (14:43–44)

After Jonathan's victory over the Philistines, King Saul for-
bade anyone within the army to eat anything until he avenged his
enemies. Jonathan didn't get the memo and he tasted some honey.
He didn't blame anyone else, and he didn't try to justify his actions.
He accepted the consequences, even if they seemed unfair. The rest
of the men in the army intervened on his behalf, sparing his life.

Great teammates aren't perfect. They will make mistakes and do
things they regret. They do not, however, hide under a rock when
their misdeeds are exposed. They don't blame other teammates.
They don't use social media as a passive-aggressive outlet. Even if the
punishment seems unfair, they accept it and learn from it.

Great Teammates Fight against Entitlement

As soon as he had finished speaking to Saul, the
soul of Jonathan was knit to the soul of David, and
Jonathan loved him as his own soul. And Saul took
him that day and would not let him return to his
father's house. (18:1–2)

This passage comes on the heels of David killing Goliath. By this
point in the story, David is pegged as the next king of Israel. None
of Saul's sons, including Jonathan, would succeed their father on the
throne. The young shepherd who had killed lions and bears—and

now Goliath—had the nation's attention. He had just moved into the starting lineup and taken Jonathan's spot.

How did Jonathan respond? He loved David as he loved himself. He committed to being one in spirit with David.

How would you respond? The disease of entitlement runs rampant in the world of sports: "I deserve this spot. I worked hard for my position. I am next in line when they graduate. I am better than they are. What they did was not that impressive."

It's so easy to become bitter at those who "steal" your spotlight or playing time. Great teammates seek to put others above themselves, especially in moments when it is most difficult to do so.

Great Teammates Don't Have a Hidden Agenda

> Then Jonathan made a covenant with David, because he loved him as his own soul. And Jonathan stripped himself of the robe that was on him and gave it to David, and his armor, and even his sword and his bow and his belt. (18:3–4)

Jonathan was *all in* on his friendship and loyalty to David. What we see in these verses is Jonathan giving up everything given to him and everything he worked for in order to help David advance. It's evident that Jonathan wasn't just trying to get on David's good side so he could leverage that position later. His words and his actions reflected his heart's desire.

Great teammates truly want what is best for others on the team. Their actions and words are not just a strategy to get back into the coach's good graces but are an overflow of a desire to see others succeed, even if it comes at a significant cost.

Great Teammates Speak Well of Their Teammates Privately

> And Jonathan spoke well of David to Saul his father and said to him, "Let not the king sin against his servant David, because he has not sinned against you, and because his deeds have brought good to you." (19:4)

As David continued to grow in popularity among the people, King Saul became increasingly jealous and wanted to kill David. This was Jonathan's chance to reclaim his spot. But he did not take the bait.

Great teammates don't lurk behind the scenes looking for an opportunity to capitalize on the misfortune of others. When necessary and appropriate, they advocate for their teammates behind closed doors. Anyone can champion a teammate in public. It takes a great teammate to do it when no one else is watching.

Great Teammates Let Their Teammates Know They Have Their Back

> Then Jonathan said to David, "Whatever you say, I will do for you." (20:4)

When David was desperate, he came to Jonathan. He knew that Saul wanted him dead. Jonathan did not say, "Good luck" or "I will keep you in my prayers." He looked his friend in the eye and said he would do anything he asked him to do.

Great teammates don't put limits on what they will do for others. They are willing to be inconvenienced to help a teammate out of a jam. This stands in stark contrast to the me-centered attitude of our sports culture. This willingness to help comes out of a growing awareness of the lengths to which Jesus went to serve and sacrifice for us. If he laid everything on the line for us, we glorify him by modeling that same sacrificial spirit in our relationships with our teammates.

Great Teammates Enter into Their Teammates' Pain

> And Jonathan rose from the table in fierce anger and ate no food the second day of the month, for he was grieved for David, because his father had disgraced him…. And as soon as the boy had gone, David rose from beside the stone heap and fell on his face to the ground and bowed three times. And they kissed one another and wept with one another, David weeping the most. (20:34, 41)

Saul finally reached his tipping point. He expressed to Jonathan his disdain for him as a son and his intentions to kill David. In a moment when he had every right to isolate himself in order to recover from the personal attacks of his father, Jonathan chose to hurt with David. At that moment, he decided to enter into his friend's pain rather than stay only in his own.

Great teammates allow themselves to enter into the pain of others. If a teammate gets injured, they imagine what it must be like to be in that person's shoes. If a teammate loses or performs poorly, they encourage their teammate and try to lift his or her spirits. Great teammates don't try to fix the problem or minimize the pain. They say things like, "I'm really sorry. I can't imagine what you're going through. What do you need from me? I'm in your corner."

Great Teammates Celebrate Their Teammates' Success

The Scriptures don't record many celebratory moments between David and Jonathan. It's pretty safe to assume, however, that when good things happened to David, Jonathan was joyfully celebrating with him.

Romans 12:15 implores believers to "rejoice with those who rejoice." Great teammates enter into the joy of others and celebrate with them.

> If he laid everything on the line for us, we glorify him by modeling that same sacrificial spirit in our relationships with our teammates.

Sometimes a teammate's success will come at the cost of your own. If you can't muster up the energy in your heart to find happiness for your teammate, it becomes an opportunity for you to confess that to the Lord and repent. An inability to celebrate others is a terrible, joy-robbing way to live.

Great teammates embrace the call to "love your neighbor as yourself," as Jesus said in Matthew 19:19. Part of loving your neighbor—and your teammates—is being happy when good fortune comes their way.

What If I Honestly Don't Like Them?

Of course, all this is easy when you like your teammates. What happens when you can't stand some of them?

You can probably envision them in your head right now. The teammate who puts on a smile in front of you but gossips and spreads lies behind your back. The teammate who doesn't work nearly as hard as you do and yet has found favor with the coaching staff. The teammate who has a flair for the dramatic and seems addicted to the sympathy of others. The list goes on.

The natural tendency is to avoid these kinds of teammates as much as possible. But what does it look like, practically, to glorify God in these hard situations? Christian athletes are called to a higher standard.

By looking at Jonathan's life, we discerned ten ways a gospel-centered teammate could act unselfishly toward others. But we need an additional approach in dealing with those teammates who consistently knock our hearts off the gospel-centered path. What are some things you can do to realign your heart in these instances?

Pray for Them

In Matthew 5:44, Jesus says to his followers, "I say to you, Love your enemies and pray for those who persecute you." I would not classify a difficult teammate as an enemy, but the principle remains the same—pray for people who don't like you and for people you don't like.

What should you pray? Ask God to move in their lives, convict them about what they're doing wrong, and open the eyes of their hearts to see the grace that's freely offered. Then look for opportunities to share the gospel with them.

Pray for Yourself

Often, the people who frustrate us most are more similar to us than we would like to think. The mirroring effect of their lives disturbs us. It's easier to vilify them than to admit our own shortcomings. The possibility exists that God may want to do more in your heart in this situation than in the teammate who is annoying you. Maybe he actually wants to change *you*. Colossians says:

> Put on then, as God's chosen ones, holy and beloved, compassionate hearts, kindness, humility, meekness, and patience, bearing with one another and, if one has a complaint against another, forgiving each other; as the Lord has forgiven you, so you also must forgive. And above all these put on love, which binds everything together in perfect harmony. (3:12–14)

Pray that God would soften your heart toward this teammate, giving you patience, compassion, and the ability to see through his or her eyes. Who knows—maybe God is using this teammate to refine you so that your character more closely mirrors Jesus.

Encourage Them

By dying to yourself and showing kindness to someone who frustrates you, you will inevitably look different from most people. Again, that's the point. Christian athletes should be a light shining in a dark world. But more importantly, you will *feel* different because you choose to walk in obedience to God instead of allowing sin to take root in your heart. (If you need ideas for how to encourage a teammate, take a look at the previous chapter.)

Forgive Them

Do you know who has every right to be frustrated with you? God. Do you know how many times a day your actions and thoughts affront his holiness? If you are like me, often. Yet how does God deal with us? Romans 5:8 says, "God shows his love for us in that while we were still sinners, Christ died for us." When did God demonstrate his love for us? Not after we cleaned up our act but while we were in the act.

We glorify God when we think and act in a way that pleases God and draws attention to who he is. There are few greater ways to do this than to forgive someone who doesn't deserve it. Colossians 3:13 says that acting like a Christian means "bearing with one another and, if one has a complaint against another, forgiving each other; as the Lord has forgiven you, so you also must forgive."

Ask for Accountability

Loving difficult teammates is challenging. As with any battle you are facing, trying to do it in isolation is only going to make it tougher. In his second letter to the Thessalonians, Paul shows his need for help:

Finally, brothers, pray for us, that the word of the
Lord may speed ahead and be honored, as happened among you, and that we may be delivered
from wicked and evil men. For not all have faith.
(3:1–2)

Inviting another person into your present challenges greatly
increases your chance of success. That's glorifying to God. What
does it look like practically? Find another teammate, friend, coach,
or parent and say something like this: "I'm really struggling with
this individual. You know how much she gets under my skin. I want
to make a better effort to love her like Jesus. Here is what I am going
to try to do: __(fill in the blank)__. Would you make it a point to
ask me how I am doing in this area once a week? Or better yet,
would you remind me before practice starts to love her like Jesus?"

In a culture that celebrates the platforms that come with public
success, your greatest influence may be on the teammates you rub
shoulders with every day. We all want to believe God has marvelous
plans for us through success in our sports. And maybe he does. But
what if he has you where you are so you can be a light to your teammates? Remember, it's ultimately about his glory, not your own.

Questions for Individual Reflection or Team Study

Who is the best teammate you have ever had? Why?

What character traits would you use to describe a great teammate?

What are some challenges of being a great teammate?

Of the ten observations the author made about Jonathan, which stood out to you the most? Why?

Of the ten, which are you already modeling well? Which do you need to work on?

Why do you think God wants us to move toward teammates we do not get along with? How does that bring him glory?

Is there a teammate right now who frustrates you? What action steps can you take from the options the author laid out?

Additional Questions for Coaches to Consider

In your role as a coach, who would you say your "teammates" are?

What does it look like as a coach to be a great teammate in practical ways?

What do other coaches need most from you?

Are there any practical adjustments you could make as a coach to begin (or continue) building a culture that encourages "great teammates"?

9

On Riding the Bench

*Things turn out best for people who make
the best of the way things turn out.*

The mark of a true athlete is the desire to compete. Sound logic and common sense tell us that no competitive athlete enjoys sitting on the sidelines. Yet the reality is that sports sometimes force us into situations where we have to sit and wait. And watch.

Sometimes a losing season or poor playoff effort prevents future competition, forcing the unfortunate majority to watch the fortunate few march toward a championship. Other times, an injury forces us to become spectators of the game we love. At some point, our body's betrayal will lead us to retirement.

Perhaps the worst way to be sidelined, however, is to hear the words "You're just not good enough." Ouch. More painful than the act of watching your team play without you is the knowledge that your coach doesn't think you have what it takes to contribute.

What does it look like for a Christian athlete to stay faithful to God and bring him glory while riding the pine?

I think it looks a lot like my friend Phoebe.

Phoebe played ice hockey and was a star in high school. Before her school had a women's program, she played with and against the boys' team. By the time she graduated, she had full-ride offers from every major Division I college that had a women's ice hockey program. Her plan in college was pretty simple: dominate, become a star, give God all the glory.

But God had a different plan for Phoebe. As she related to me recently:

> God saw right through my plan. He saw what I couldn't see: my selfish pride and desire to glorify myself getting in the way of me ever really making him known to people. So, in a way I didn't expect, he took away that one thing that my identity, value, and self-worth were wrapped up in: my sport.

Though she was fully capable of dominating in her sport, she never got the opportunity. Though she got some opportunities to compete for her school, Phoebe spent much of her college career watching her team—a team that would win two national championships while she was there—from the bench.

She recalls the first time the coach told her she wouldn't be suiting up for the game:

> I can still *vividly* remember the first game that I was told I wouldn't be in the lineup. I remember sitting in the stands in my street clothes watching my

teammates warm up and questioning for literally the first time in my life whether I was good enough at my sport. It really hurt. It was then that God began to slowly open my eyes to the reality that, while I had always spoken about (and believed) that my identity was in my relationship with Jesus, it turned out that my heart belonged to something else: the self-worth that I had cultivated through my success as a hockey player. As the season wore on, I struggled almost daily with self-confidence on the ice.

Phoebe went to Athletes in Action's Ultimate Training Camp and experienced God breaking down her heart's idols of self-worth and identity being wrapped up in sports success. She remembers God whispering to her heart that he wanted her right where he had her to serve her teammates by loving them and competing hard for them, regardless of her status as a hockey player.

There are (at least) six things we can learn from Phoebe's experience on the bench.

You Don't Need to Play to Glorify God

Phoebe's desire and ability to glorify God were not stunted by her time on the bench. Honoring the Lord through sports is not contingent on one's ability to actually see time on the playing field—or in Phoebe's case, the ice. In fact, sitting out can shed light on what you truly value.

As Jesus says:

If you love those who love you, what benefit is that to you? For even sinners love those who love them. And if you do good to those who do good to you, what benefit is that to you? For even sinners do the same. And if you lend to those from whom you expect to receive, what credit is that to you? Even sinners lend to sinners, to get back the same amount. But love your enemies, and do good, and lend, expecting nothing in return, and your reward will be great, and you will be sons of the Most High, for he is kind to the ungrateful and the evil. (Luke 6:32–35)

Of course, Jesus is not talking about sports. But he *is* pointing out a principle about how God works that transfers well into sports. Jesus says if you love others only when it's convenient for you, it's not really love. If you give to people you know will give back in return, it's not really generosity.

For athletes, I think the principle might sound something like this: "If you seek to glorify God only when you're on the field and things are going well, what benefit is that to you? Everyone gives God glory when the chips fall in their favor. Seek to glorify him in the valleys—and on the bench."

Colossians 3:23–24 doubles down on this truth and gives us a great trajectory for moving forward: "Whatever you do, work heartily, as for the Lord and not for men, knowing that from the Lord you will receive the inheritance as your reward. You are serving the Lord Christ."

You glorify God when you work hard and when your motivation for doing so is because you are seeking to please the Lord. If your coach decides not to play you, make sure you've practiced so well and so hard that it's about your level of skill, not your work ethic or attitude.

Speaking of attitude, you can still be frustrated internally and have a great attitude externally. How do you do this? By looking for ways to be thankful in the middle of your frustration. First Thessalonians 5:18 says, "Give thanks in all circumstances; for this is the will of God in Christ Jesus for you."

Be a thankful athlete. Be known as hope-filled, humble, and thankful. Don't allow yourself to become lumped among the complainers. Vocally express thanks to your coach for a great workout, and humbly ask what you can do to keep improving.

Athlete, God's ability to receive glory is not contingent on sports success. It starts with what's going on in your heart.

Don't Fake It with God

Glorifying God while riding the bench involves understanding that it's okay to be frustrated when our expectations are not met. We have to make it a habit to run toward God as we are—not how we think he wants us to be. In the world of sport, you're supposed to put on a brave face and look the part of champion. But in the kingdom of God, your brokenness and disappointment can pave the road to fullness of life.

It's okay to feel frustrated that you are not getting the playing time you want. Most likely, you have put in countless hours of training. You have endured grueling practices and weight room sessions. You've expended the time, effort, and energy it takes to run with the start-ers—or to get at least *some* playing time. Part of being a competitive athlete is having an appropriate level of confidence in your abilities.

Disappointment is always birthed from unmet expectations:

1. You put in the work.
2. You expected to play.
3. You're not playing.
4. Hence, the disappointment.

Don't feel guilty for having an emotional response to an unmet expectation. There's nothing wrong with being frustrated about your predicament. In fact, one could argue that *not* being frustrated would be wrong. Having emotions is part of the human experience. It's how God wired us. Moses felt insecure. Jeremiah felt betrayed. David cried. Jesus wept.

Welcome to the family. But what you do with your negative emotions will help you honor God in the middle of your circum-stances. And the first thing you can do with those emotions is to be honest with him.

Our God has uniquely designed us as relational beings who are most satisfied when we are connected to our Creator. That means we communicate with him—regardless of our circumstance.

I've been married for fifteen years. My wife is my best friend. Do you want to know one of the secrets to a successful marriage? Communication. If I want a thriving relationship with my wife, I need to be honest with her when I am having a bad day or when I am frustrated. The whole "fake it 'til you make it" advice is a great recipe for an awful relationship. True intimacy requires honesty when the circumstances are less than ideal.

It's the same with our relationship with God. In fact, how you respond to God when times get tough is a great measuring stick for where your relationship is with him. Do you run *to* him or *from* him?

Chase Joy While Deep in Disappointment

Phoebe experienced joy by encouraging her teammates to be the best version of themselves and by pushing them on the ice—sometimes at the cost of her own playing time.

"I wanted to honor Jesus with my effort," she said.

Shouldn't lack of playing time rob you of the very joy you could have experienced playing the game you love? Phoebe loves the game of hockey—and she is really good at it. But she refused to let her joy become dependent on circumstances.

You can have joy in any situation that involves you not playing. But you need to *rightly* pursue it.

If I'm playing baseball and want to get from first base to third base but neglect to move toward second base at any point, I am not going to get there. Despite my intention, my direction actually determines my destination. In the same way, if you want joy, you need to know where to find it.

Athlete, do you want to know the secret of where to find joy?

Paul shared the road map with us in Philippians:

> I know what it is to be in need, and I know what it
> is to have plenty. I have learned the secret of being
> content in any and every situation, whether well

fed or hungry, whether living in plenty or in want. I
can do all this through him who gives me strength.
(4:12–13 NIV)

Joy is available to you because it's dependent on and found in
the person and work of Jesus Christ.

Phoebe learned the secret of being content, regardless of the
situation. Her joy was in Christ. The same joy is available to you.
If you chase after Jesus while you're injured or sitting on the bench,
you will find the joy your heart longs to experience.

Have a Vision beyond Your Sport

You glorify God from the bench when you're open to the possibility
that God may have you on the team for purposes other than being
the star player on a championship team. When Phoebe realized that
her purpose for being on the bench was to serve her teammates, her
perspective shifted.

> You glorify God from the bench when
> you're open to the possibility that God
> may have you on the team for purposes
> other than being the star player on a
> championship team.

Often, what gets us through the pain is proper perspective.
Phoebe understood that her purpose went beyond the sport she
played. She rightly prioritized people above the game. If her primary
purpose had been starting on the hockey team, the lack of playing

time would have broken her spirit. But her higher calling allowed her to persevere through admittedly difficult times.

We'll talk about this more in chapter 12, but this is a good spot to prime the pump for that conversation. You can impact others whether you're on the field leading the team or in training room/ locker room conversations. In fact, the locker room may be your most effective arena for glorifying God. And if you find yourself riding the bench, I want to encourage you to take advantage of the opportunity.

You don't need to be a professional Christian (like a pastor) to have a ministry. If you are in Christ, you have a mission field. Again, we can look to the apostle Paul here:

> If anyone is in Christ, he is a new creation. The old has passed away; behold, the new has come. All this is from God, who through Christ reconciled us to himself and gave us the ministry of reconciliation; that is, in Christ God was reconciling the world to himself, not counting their trespasses against them, and entrusting to us the message of reconciliation. Therefore, we are ambassadors for Christ, God making his appeal through us. We implore you on behalf of Christ, be reconciled to God. (2 Cor. 5:17–20)

If you were asked to describe yourself using a word that started with the letter *a*, what would you choose? I'm guessing you might choose *athlete*. But you have a better identity in Christ. You are an *ambassador*. Phoebe understood that, above all else, she was an ambassador for Christ. Do you?

When you see yourself as an ambassador, the people around you become your ministry. Phoebe began to see her teammates, coaches, trainers, and support staff as her mission field.

She started college assuming her platform as a star athlete would allow her to minister to fans all over the country as she redirected praise back to God. But she learned that her primary focus and platform came from within the walls of her college facilities.

Ambassador, use this season of not playing to refocus your attention off of yourself and onto your teammates and coaches. Look to serve them. Pray for them. God may just have you in this position to make his appeal to them through you. Will you let him?

Trust That God Knows What He Is Doing

Phoebe's confidence in who God is allowed her to stay at the college she had committed to instead of transferring when things got hard. Even if she didn't like what God was up to, she trusted that he knew more than she did.

Wherever you are at and whatever reasons that exist for you not playing, I want to encourage you to trust that God is going to use this for his glory if you partner with him in the process. The apostle Paul says, "Not only so, but we also glory in our sufferings, because we know that suffering produces perseverance; perseverance, character; and character, hope" (Rom. 5:3–4 NIV).

Now, I am definitely not comparing the sufferings of Paul with Phoebe's (or your) lack of playing time. I know she wouldn't either. Suffering can come in thousands of forms, and it really doesn't matter what type of suffering you're facing, because the potential outcome of any suffering can be the same. The progression of suffering to perseverance to character to hope is the process Phoebe went through—even if it was at a different level than Paul's. It may be the process you're going through as well.

Trust that God knows what he is doing in your life. This lack of playing time is part of his plan for you. Again, it's okay if that stings to hear. But understand that your situation is not a surprise to God. If you allow it to, it will produce perseverance. That perseverance will grow your character. And that character will help you hope.

You can cling to the truth echoed by Paul in Romans 8:28: "We know that for those who love God all things work together for good, for those who are called according to his purpose."

Athlete, God has his glory and your good at the forefront of his mind. Those two goals are not an either-or deal. It's both-and. But our natural definition of *good* must give way to God's definition.

Fight against Prosperity Gospel Mentality

Phoebe's team ended up winning back-to-back national championships during her remaining two years. I need to caution you against drawing this unbiblical connection: After God tested Phoebe by making her ride the bench, she proved faithful and trusted in his plan, and he rewarded that faith with two national titles. This is dangerous theology.

When we choose to believe that God can be glorified and pleased only through success, we believe a false gospel. It's one commonly referred to as the prosperity gospel.

The prosperity gospel says, "If I trust in God and have enough faith, he will reward me with earthly blessings like health, wealth, and success."

Within the context of sports, that means if you lose, it's because you didn't pray hard enough, or sinned earlier in the week, or didn't have enough faith. The prosperity gospel teaches that you would have won had you done the right things or had more faith that God would bring you out on top.

 Learn how you can get better at what you are already good at.

It also means that if you start obeying harder and having more faith, then God will look down from the heavens and reward you with the playing time you desire. But God cannot be manipulated. God is not a vending machine that spits out blessings if you put in the right quantity of faith. The Bible shows us that trials and suffering will come our way. God may end up making a way for you to play—and by his grace, he may allow you to experience great success—but it will be because of his sovereign plan, not because your behavior convinced him it was time or because your obedience forced his hand.

If you are riding the bench, here are three more things to do.

Ask Your Coach Why You Are Not Playing

I'm not suggesting that you storm into the office and demand answers. I'm talking about taking the initiative to get something on the coach's schedule so you can humbly ask, "What can I do to get better?"

Proverbs 10:17 says, "Whoever heeds instruction is on the path to life, but he who rejects reproof leads others astray." Ask questions. Learn how you can get better at what you are already good at. Also identify the weak areas that need improvement and are preventing you from getting on the field.

The easier option is to avoid your coaches and gossip behind their backs to your friends and teammates. You know it already, but I will still say it: that's a sinful approach that dishonors both your coaches and God.

> God is not a vending machine that spits out blessings if you put in the right quantity of faith.

One of the markers of humility is taking on the posture of a student. When you show the desire to be a continual learner, you honor your coach as the teacher—and glorify God.

Confess Entitlement

You may want to take a deep breath before you read the next sentence.

You are not entitled to any playing time.

That's sounds harsh, but it's the reality. Your coach's job is dependent on whether your team wins. Period. If your coach does not think your talent level is at a place where you can help the team get a W, then he or she is under no obligation to put you on the field.

You may have been the best athlete on your team before you got here. You may have been a star. But your current coach is not obligated to play you because of your highlight reel.

What needs to be pressed against here is the "I deserve" mentality that erodes your attitude like a cancer. Yes, this is blunt. But so is God's response to pride throughout the Bible (see Prov. 16:5 and 8:13, for example). And an "I deserve" heart posture equals pride.

If you sense this in your life, confess it quickly to God and ask Him to help change your heart.

Don't Transfer to Another School the Second You Aren't Playing

God may have something for you in this season of waiting that involves something better than splinters in your rear end. Don't hit the eject button just yet. There could be a variety of reasons you are not playing, but I want to implore you to look for purpose that transcends the playing field in this difficult season. God has you in this spot—don't waste it.

Look for ways to affirm your teammates who are in front of you in the pecking order for playing time—and directly behind you. Be the loudest and most encouraging voice they hear every single day. In most cases, the growth you will experience from becoming a varsity level advocate for your teammates will far surpass the benefits you might get from transferring.

And who knows—your coach may even notice and reward you for it.

Questions for Individual Reflection or Team Study

Describe a time when you were not able to see the playing field. How did that experience make you feel?

How did that time impact your relationship with God?

Describe one or two things from that experience that grew you as an individual or allowed you to impact a teammate or coach.

Does any part of Phoebe's story resonate with you? Which parts?

If God wants his glory and your good, how would you define what God thinks is good? How might it be different than how the rest of the world defines it?

Who on your team right now is struggling with not getting playing time? How can you come alongside them in this season of their lives to encourage them and point them toward God?

Additional Questions for Coaches to Consider

What was the most difficult benching you ever had to do as a coach?

When you bench an athlete, what do you typically say?

What do you think it looks like to bench an athlete in a way that Jesus would do it?

Describe the different reasons you would bench an athlete. Are there any benchings that you regret? Why?

How can you reward a player riding the bench with something other than playing time?

10

On Gray Areas

An honorable defeat is better than a dishonorable victory.

Millard Fillmore

We aim at what is honorable not only in the
Lord's sight but also in the sight of man.

2 Corinthians 8:21

Brian Davis walked toward the green in the 2010 Heritage Classic. He had just tied Jim Furyk on the seventy-second hole to force a sudden-death playoff. But before he started to line up his putt, he called over the officials to talk about his previous shot.

"I didn't feel anything, but I'm pretty sure that I saw that one reed move. I could be wrong because of the wind," Davis said.[1]

The officials looked at the replay and determined Davis' club had not hit the reed. They decided to take one more look in super slow motion. It turned out that Davis was right. His club had hit a reed on his backswing.

The rule book identifies a reed like that one as a "loose impediment," and according to rule 23 of the USGA's *Rules of Golf,* loose impediments can't be moved. His club had moved it. The result would be a two-stroke penalty. Nobody had seen it, and Davis hadn't felt it. But he thought he might have seen the reed move a little, so he self-reported it to the officials. Furyk went on to win the tournament.

Davis later estimated that the loss cost him close to $2 million. It was not just the tournament's prize money on the line but also an entrance into the Masters and endorsement bonuses. Davis said:

> But it's not so important that you cheat to achieve it. Golfers are expected to police themselves. It's in the gentleman's tradition of the game. It's what makes our sport unique. I'm a fan of the Arsenal Football Club and my father-in-law is Ray Clemence, who was a goalkeeper for Liverpool and England, so I know it's not the same in other sports. I'm not happy when a player goes down in the box after barely being brushed by a defender, but I know it's part of football's gamesmanship. It's not the same in golf. Even for anyone to *think* you're a cheater is horrible.[2]

Part of the Game?

With the politeness of a golfer, Davis refers to how a soccer player might act like he took a bullet to gain an advantage on the field, calling it "part of football's gamesmanship." But what about other sports?

Is it okay to steal signs in baseball or for pitchers to retaliate? What about holding a defensive lineman when the referee isn't looking? Is it okay to cut the wooded corner of the cross-country course if everyone ahead of you is cutting it? How about running up the score on a weak opponent? If you jump offsides or the ball hits you last before going out of bounds, is it just part of the game to point at the opposition as if they're to blame? All these scenarios fall under the category of gray areas within each sport's culture.

So, what's a gray area? The *Cambridge English Dictionary* defines a gray area as "a situation that is not clear or where the rules are not known."[3] In sports, the rules of the game are generally well-defined and well-known by the athletes. Usually, an athlete can't claim ignorance when it comes to rules. Sometimes, however, we run into a situation in sports that isn't quite so clear, like running up the score. There's no written rule against something like that, so it's a gray area to some extent. (Most would agree that while it may not go against the rules, it certainly violates the spirit of the game and is unsportsmanlike.)

Another example of a gray area is when we see a basketball player flop or embellish some contact to try to get a favorable call from the officials. In the NBA, flopping is illegal, and everyone knows that. But some players still try to get away with it.

A gray area in sports can be described in one of two ways:

1. It's truly a situation where there are no clearly defined rules, like running up the score or tanking the rest of the season to get a better draft pick. It's not strictly prohibited but is certainly frowned upon.

2. It's a situation in which the rules are most likely understood yet can be manipulated, exploited, or ignored to gain a tactical advantage. Each sport has some cultural norms that are understood by the players. Whether a tactic is blatantly against the rules or just part of the game, players sometimes seek to exploit these gray areas to achieve an advantage.

Each potential gray area has been debated extensively. I don't want to tackle this issue at the ground level, attempting to work my way through the positives and negatives on each side for every situation. Instead, I want to provide a big-picture view along with some questions that will help us respond to each gray area within our particular sport in a way that honors and glorifies God.

Passive Obedience versus Active Obedience

Passive obedience is when you play the game by the rules but you don't think about it at the moment. You have been trained to play the game correctly, and in the heat of competition the overflow of your training enables you to compete within the set of rules without giving it a second thought. That's glorifying to God. The natural ability to play with a high level of integrity is the north star we want to look to as Christian athletes.

But what happens when playing by the rules doesn't come naturally? What do we do when faced with the option of valuing victory over integrity? That's where active obedience comes in. Active obedience in sports means you have to make a choice about what's right and what's wrong. It requires you to think and act. What do you do on the cross-country course where spectators don't have access? If the other runners all cut the same corner, do you do it too or take a stand and put yourself at a disadvantage?

How can we make the wise decision to play with integrity? Here are a few important questions to ask yourself when faced with a gray area in your sport:

Is what I am doing considered part of the game, or is it outright shady? Romans 12:2, which talks about not being "conformed to this world," applies here. If what you're doing is shady, stop doing it. I think what needs to be taken seriously here is the line between shady, which is bordering on flat-out cheating, and how the game is actually played. But the line is extremely ... gray.

Pitching at someone's head is shady. Giving another runner a sharp elbow so he or she goes off the edge of the track or lane is shady. Purposefully cutting off a runner so he or she can't pass seems shady, but it's actually a regular tactical maneuver in track and field.

Doing the right thing may mean forfeiting a tactical advantage, but if you do so, you will look different from competitors who are willing to forfeit their integrity in a desperate attempt to win at all costs. The godly virtue of integrity applies to the sports arena just as much as anywhere else.

Here are a few additional questions to help you think through gray areas.

Is what I am doing against the written and unwritten rules? If it is, stop doing it.

Am I aware that what I am doing is against the rules, or am I doing it by accident? If you are aware, you need to repent and maybe even ask for forgiveness. In any case, stop doing it.

Has anyone ever gotten a foul, penalty, or disqualification for doing what I am doing? If so, stop doing it.

Has anyone ever communicated to me that what I am doing is not right? If so, stop doing it.

If I get caught doing this by a spectator or in a slow-motion replay, will I feel convicted? You have the Holy Spirit living in you. If you feel convicted, the probable cause is that he wants you to feel convicted. Stop doing it.

Do I sense in my heart a conviction to stop doing this? Again, if you are a Christian, you have the Holy Spirit living within you. The conviction is coming from somewhere, most likely him. Stop doing it.

Were You Speeding?

Those last two questions remind me of driving down a road where the speed limit is 55 mph. If I am driving 56 mph, am I breaking the law? Technically yes. But, as a middle-aged dad driving a minivan full of kids, I am not going to get pulled over. If I pass a cop going 56 mph, I won't even look in the rearview mirror to see if he is chasing me down.

Now, if I drive by him going anywhere above 62, I start to get nervous. I'm tapping the brakes, slowing back to 55, and checking my mirror. If he doesn't follow me, I know I've gotten away with something.

What does this have to do with sports? Often, gray areas in sport are like speed limits. They are put in place as a guideline for us to follow, but there is wiggle room to break them and nobody, not even the official, would think twice. But if you do something in your sport and you need to look over to see if the official is going to call you on it, that is probably the evidence you need (thanks a lot, Holy Spirit) that you're trying to get away with something you know is wrong.

All this matters because the Bible says God created us in his image. The implications of this reality are far-reaching. One implication is that we are to image God by acting like him.

 Play your sport within the set of rules prescribed, and you will bring glory to God.

Genesis 1:2 gives us a glimpse of how God works: "The earth was without form and void, and darkness was over the face of the deep. And the Spirit of God was hovering over the face of the waters." Verse 3 says, "And God said, 'Let there be light,' and there was light." God stared into the chaos and created order.

What does that look like in sports? Simply put, we must follow the rules of the game. We should compete by the rules all the time because they express what is orderly, fair, and just. As an image-bearer of the most high God, are you acting like him by bringing order, or are you contributing to the chaos? When we image his character, we glorify who he is.

Do you remember the definition of giving glory to God? It's thinking and acting in a way that pleases God and draws attention to who he is. When we choose to operate with integrity in every way possible, we glorify our Creator.

With respect to gray areas in sports, bearing the image of God means we place a higher premium on being obedient to him than on being successful at the expense of our integrity. How we act reveals our priorities. It almost sounds too simple. Play your sport within the set of rules prescribed, and you will bring glory to God.

When faced with an opportunity to bend the rules, you have two options:

1. Bend the rules to bring glory to yourself.
2. Obey the rules to bring glory to God.

The way a Christian athlete responds to gray areas can set him or her apart from the rest of the world. It's one of the reasons being obedient to God in all circumstances within our sport can be so impactful. When we act in countercultural ways, people take notice. Our influence often grows as a result of our obedience.

Two Words of Caution

In an article on sportsmanship, Ed Uszynski wrote:

> Doing the right thing doesn't mean you'll come out on top of the scoreboard. We can't make a deal with God or demand a pact whose contractual obligations read something like "If I do the right thing, you (God) will make sure I win the game." What you can be assured of when you live surrendered to God's standards is His favor extended toward you in any number of other ways: peace in the midst of trials, guilt-free living, wisdom to say the right thing, grace for each moment of the day, the contentment that comes from being in his will. You may win

games too, but wins and losses in the Kingdom of
God look far different than they do on the sports
page. God evaluates winners and losers according
to a completely different scoring system. His desires
are not displayed through us by tallying numbers
on a board, but in choosing righteousness, justice,
and godly character when faced with opportunities
to do so.[4]

Of course, doing the right thing can be difficult because we're
often tempted to protect our own kingdom instead of building his.
Nevertheless, integrity never goes out of style in God's economy, and
he will bless our obedience in one way or another.

Another caution for athletes who take a hard line on gray areas
is the propensity to become prideful. This can take a couple different
forms.

First, we can compare ourselves to other athletes, teammates, or
competitors who are not striving for the same level of integrity that
we are. This comparison game inevitably leads to thinking we are
better than the person next to us. You may be choosing a better path,
but believing you are more righteous than someone else is dangerous. It's also sinful. The joy received from playing the game with the
highest possible level of integrity ought to come from knowing you
are glorifying your Father, not from feeling like you are better than
everyone else.

The second form our pride can take is anger—anger directed at
those who do not choose to play with the same high level of integrity. If somebody takes a shortcut, bends the rules, or cheats in some

way, it is okay to be frustrated. Being angry is the right response to injustice. God has hardwired us to reflect his image, and when an injustice occurs, a frustrated response is a good and right response.

That being said, the bad anger I'm referring to asks, "If I can play by the rules, why can't they?" It says, "Look, I'm doing it right. They should be able to do it right too." That's pride. There's a big difference between being frustrated by injustice and feeling resentful because others can't measure up to your standards.

 Integrity never goes out of style in God's economy, and he will bless our obedience in one way or another.

So how should Christian athletes approach gray areas within their sports? With the highest possible standard of integrity. Doing so glorifies God. And your integrity, empowered by God's grace in your life, may give you opportunities to explain why you choose to play the way you do despite competing in a culture that values winning above everything else.

Questions for Individual Reflection or Team Study

What are the gray areas in your sport?

What is the shadiest thing you have ever gotten away with in your sport?

After reading this chapter, is there anything you are currently doing while competing that you feel convicted about?

What is the connection between God being a "God of order" and us following the rules of our sport?

How would you define *integrity*?

If you do the right thing at the expense of gaining a competitive advantage, do you believe God will reward you? Why or why not? What form might any reward take?

Additional Questions for Coaches to Consider

How do you coach your athletes in the gray areas of your sport?

Do you lean more toward an integrity-at-all-costs or a win-at-all-costs mindset?

Prayerfully make a list of everyone who would be impacted if you got caught on the wrong side of a gray area.

Looking at the list, is getting a win worth sacrificing your integrity and potentially your reputation in relationship to all these people?

What are some practical ways you can hold yourself and your fellow coaches accountable in these areas?

11

On Coaches

This is the secret of being content: to learn and accept that
we live daily by God's unmerited favor given through
Christ, and that we can respond to any and every situation
by His divine enablement through the Holy Spirit.

Jerry Bridges, *The Practice of Godliness*

The blog post wasn't particularly long, coming in at just under 650 words. While it wasn't written poorly, it also wasn't written by someone who was overly concerned about sentence flow or grammar. This was a flat-out rant. And it struck a nerve.

On August 15, 2016, Madison Trout, a college basketball player, hit Send on a blog post that would resonate with hundreds of thousands of athletes across the country. It was called "The Coach That Killed My Passion," and the subtitle was "An open letter to the coach that made me hate a sport I once loved."

The blog spread virally through social media channels, with each additional like and share serving as affirmation that other individuals had felt similar disdain for how their coaches treated them. The post shed light on an all-too-familiar narrative—a coaching style that neglects encouragement and motivates from fear. Trout wanted to say this to the coach: "Making me feel bad about myself doesn't make me want to play and work hard for you, whether in the classroom or on the court."[1]

This issue is personal for me as well. My first cross-country practice in college started with me and all the other newbies on top of a picnic table. The rest of the team circled us. The coach then walked up to each of us and tugged our shorts down, revealing to everyone whether we were wearing boxers or briefs. It was humiliating.

Four years later, I found myself in the ACC championship cross-country race. With two miles to go, I heard my coach yell out to me, "Brian, you're killing us!" To his credit, I *was* killing our team. Simply pointing out the reality, however, was not motivating. I have to wonder how I would have finished if he had yelled something to encourage me.

I've also sat across from countless athletes at every level who have struggled with their relationship with their coaches.

If a coach's ultimate goal is to achieve an optimal level of play, we need to admit that sometimes fear and shame can be effective motivators. It is unwise and ineffective in the long-term, at least, to reinforce an athlete's fear of failure with more fear tactics. Instead, constructive and encouraging coaching is a much better way to bring about the results coaches want.

I have found in my own parenting that sometimes the most effective strategy is to threaten to take away something my child loves if he or she doesn't change an unhealthy behavior. If this becomes a habitual strategy, however, I am no longer acting like a parent; I begin to resemble a tyrant.

There is a time and a place when fear is an appropriate means of motivating, but what my experience has taught me is that most of the time, fear and shame get wielded as a weapon, not as an instrument of change. I've analyzed four reasons why I think some coaches drift toward motivating by fear and, in the process, make their athletes' lives miserable. As you will learn shortly, however, none of these reasons gives you a license to fight back.

It's worth noting that most Christian coaches I have interacted with over the years have worked hard to implement a coaching philosophy grounded in love and biblical principles. This chapter highlights the darker side of coaching in order to show the posture a Christian athlete should have in response—because, unfortunately, many Christian athletes do not play for coaches who value a biblical model of coaching.

Fear of Failure

One of the most challenging realities for coaches is the fact that their paychecks depend on the performances of the athletes they coach. For the vast majority of coaches, that means their ability to pay the mortgage and put food on the table rests in the hands and feet of the young men and women they coach. If they don't win early and often, they could be out and replaced. Such a fear might come out in the way they coach.

Insecurity

Coaching is a dangerous profession for an individual who struggles with insecurity. Why? People who are insecure are constantly looking for validation from others. A quick Google search of specific coaches shows you what they are ultimately measured by—the number of wins and losses they have accrued over the years.

For someone who struggles with insecurity—and that's probably an overwhelming majority of both coaches and athletes alike—the win-loss record becomes an extension of their identity. So when the team struggles or an individual athlete underperforms, coaches have a tendency to lash out.

It's a defense mechanism that, in my experience, is often reactive, not premeditated. In the unpredictable world of sports, we should hardly be surprised when our coaches respond to our performances in ways that we would deem unhelpful. If we desire grace for our shortcomings in sport, perhaps we would be wise to lead by example and extend that same grace to our coaches.

Immaturity

Some coaches lack the ability to control their emotions in the heat of the moment. This is unfortunate. Athletes don't get a free pass for being out of control on the field. Likewise, coaches should not get a free pass for uncontrolled outbursts under the guise of motivation.

I have been involved in sports at some level for the past twenty-five years. One thing I have noticed is that most coaches who motivate their athletes by fear are not trying to motivate at all; they are unloading their own anger, fear, and shame issues at the easiest target.

I get this, even as a parent. When my kid spills milk on the carpet, my gut reaction is to yell, "If you do that again, I will never give you milk again!" Is that motivating by fear? Sure. At my core, however, I'm just trying to feel better and regain a sense of control by unleashing my anger on the easiest target. It doesn't make me an awful parent or the world's worst dad. It just means that, in a moment when things didn't go my way, I reacted in sin.

My job at that moment is to be the adult and rise above my frustration and assess what is the best course of action to take for the betterment of my child. The same should be said of coaches who see an athlete make a mistake or underperform. They should ask themselves, *What will help this athlete grow?* But again, sometimes the heat of the moment gets the best of coaches—even the elite ones.

Power

While insecurity and immaturity use fear reactively, the desire to leverage power over a vulnerable athlete is often a proactive tactic. Every coach in authority over a player—especially in nonprofessional environments—understands intuitively that he or she has power over that player. The coach controls whether you are on the team at all as well as your playing time and, to some extent, your overall experience. Often, players feel powerless to fight back when they are verbally, emotionally, or even physically abused by a coach. Such cases (and coaches) are rare. But they still exist.

A Higher Standard

This book is not primarily for coaches. It is written for athletes— specifically, the Christian athlete. And Christian athletes are called by God to a higher standard. Regardless of whether your coach motivates through fear or shame, insecurity, immaturity, or power, your response should remain consistent with how the Bible instructs us to act when we're under someone else's authority.

Do all things without grumbling or disputing,
that you may be blameless and innocent, children
of God without blemish in the midst of a crooked
and twisted generation, among whom you shine as
lights in the world. (Phil. 2:14–15)

Your coach may be a jerk who treats you unfairly. Your coach
may purposely try to make your life miserable because he doesn't
like you. Your coach may be doing the best she can with her own
stressors and wounds. But guess what? Jesus was in a similar situation. He was falsely accused and betrayed. He did not fight back.
He did not argue. He did not complain. He did not rant on his
blog about his unfair predicament or lash out on social media. He
stayed faithful and obedient to God throughout a horrifically unfair
situation. We would do well to follow his lead.

It's our job as God's lights in this dark world to submit to authority, stay positive, and display the life and love of Jesus in harsh and
unfair situations. Complaining and demanding that we get what
we think we deserve shows an immature understanding of how we
ought to respond to the authority over us.

Athlete, save yourself the mental energy of figuring out all the
reasons your coach is wrong and you are right. Your biblical mandate
in these instances is to faithfully submit to your coach, even if his or
her methods are less than ideal. The evidence in your case may very
well prove that your coach is acting like a jerk, but it is a dangerous
leap to believe that God is more concerned with your coach's actions
than with yours.

We need a faith-filled, submissive response to a coach who insists upon a coaching method that brings frustration. What does it look like to glorify God by how we respond, inwardly and outwardly, to our coaches?

Inward Realignments

I understand that we all want practical ways to glorify God. But if we have bitter and frustrated hearts, we are missing out on fully glorifying God and we are robbing ourselves of joy in the process. Two realignments need to take place inside us.

Shift Expectations

I heard this life-changing truth a few years ago from Pastor Matt Chandler, and it has helped me in every category of my life: "Every disappointment in life is a result of unmet expectations." This does not mean always lowering expectations—though in some instances that can be beneficial—but it does mean your expectations need to be realistic. Your coach's job is to win. The decisions he or she makes along the way will be efforts toward that end.

At the end of the day, *your* performance determines your coach's future. Your coach's job is not to be your friend, your biggest cheerleader, or your counselor. You need to get rid of those expectations. You will free yourself up from a lot of inevitable disappointment if you make yourself release these unrealistic expectations. Those needs for a friend, a cheerleader, or a counselor can and should be filled by your friends, your parents, and your teammates—not your coach.

Shift Perspective

The other internal change that needs to happen is to shift the object of our obedience from our coach to the Lord. Paul encourages workers (and athletes) to render "service with a good will as to the Lord and not to man, knowing that whatever good anyone does, this he will receive back from the Lord, whether he is a bondservant or is free" (Eph. 6:7–8). Paul is encouraging his readers to recognize that God is the one we are serving.

We see a similar exhortation in Colossians:

> Bondservants, obey in everything those who are your earthly masters, not by way of eye-service, as people-pleasers, but with sincerity of heart, fearing the Lord. Whatever you do, work heartily, as for the Lord and not for men, knowing that from the Lord you will receive the inheritance as your reward. You are serving the Lord Christ. (3:22–24)

How does Paul encourage the Christian bondservants of his time? He pleads with them to look past their earthly authorities to their heavenly authority. He asks them to work "as for the Lord" because they are really "serving the Lord Christ."

As you think ahead to practices and competitions, seek to be obedient to the Lord through humble submission to your coach. Life was a lot tougher for first-century Christian bondservants than it is for you as an athlete under the authority of a coach, yet the call to submission remains the same. Athlete, honor the Lord by honoring your coach, even if the coach is undeserving—*especially* if the coach is undeserving.

As you wrestle with realigning your expectations and perspective in this area, here are some practical action steps you can begin incorporating into your life to glorify God through the way you interact with your coach.

 Athlete, honor the Lord by honoring your coach.

Work Hard

Colossians 3:23–24 gives us even more wise and necessary counsel: "Whatever you do, work heartily, as for the Lord and not for men, knowing that from the Lord you will receive the inheritance as your reward. You are serving the Lord Christ."

Before I joined staff with Athletes in Action, I was a volunteer assistant coach for the women's track and cross-country team at the University of Wisconsin for almost three years. I had the opportunity to help coach a few All-Americans and a couple of future Olympians. But my favorite athlete to coach never competed in a varsity race.

Her name was Jackie. She was part of the team Bible study and noticeably prioritized her faith. Jackie lacked the natural running talent that many of the girls possessed. Yes, all of them worked hard—you have to if you want to run at that level. But Jackie's extraordinary work ethic and drive had us coaches secretly rooting for her success.

Extraordinary work ethic should be a foundational trait for a Christian athlete.

As I've said, you glorify God when you work hard and your motivation for doing so is to please the Lord. And take it from someone who coached for three years and interacts with coaches on a regular basis: though your coaches may not reward you with playing time, they are secretly rooting for your success more than you realize.

When You Screw Up, Own It

I have listened to countless athletes ranting to me about a coach who reamed them out after a game or practice. I listen as they justify why their coach was wrong and they were right. When they're done, I gently remind them of the opportunity and responsibility before them as a Christian athlete: give respect, express humility, and practice self-control.

All three of those are biblical trajectories for an individual who is under the authority of someone else. What's at issue in these interactions with your coach is not convincing a jury of your peers that you were right but learning how to humbly submit to those in a position of authority over you. Getting into a habit of owning your shortcomings in sport will go a long way for you in life, when the stakes are much higher.

You will perform poorly at times, and when you do, there's a chance your coach will let you have it verbally. This is not the time to lash back with excuses, even if they are true.

Having a bad practice or a miserable competition is not a sin that you need to confess. But the expectation placed on you by your coach demands a certain level of excellence. When your level of play does not match that expectation, own it. Don't talk back. Don't sulk or pout. Tell your coach you know you need to—and can—do better next time.

 Getting into a habit of owning your shortcomings in sport will go a long way for you in life, when the stakes are much higher.

Honor Your Coaches When They Are Not Present

Proverbs 18:8 warns, "The words of a whisperer are like delicious morsels; they go down into the inner parts of the body." In his book *Resisting Gossip*, Matthew Mitchell offers a helpful definition: "Sinful gossip is bearing bad news behind someone's back out of a bad heart."[2]

Listen, I know how strong the temptation is to unload on a coach behind his or her back. I was often guilty of this. It's the easy way out. It's the natural way people operate. However, Christian athletes are called to stand out from the crowd, to look different. I wish I would have heeded the words of Ephesians 4:29: "Let no corrupting talk come out of your mouths, but only such as is good for building up, as fits the occasion, that it may give grace to those who hear."

Remember Phoebe from the chapter about riding the bench? While she had ample opportunities to complain about her coaches, she refused to talk about them behind their backs. When I asked for her motivation for doing so, she said, "I wanted to be consistent and honor the Lord in both my words and my actions. And I needed to trust that my coaches were doing their job and making decisions for the good of our team."

Pray for Your Coach

I once had an issue with someone who held a position of authority over me. I struggled with bitterness and resentment toward this person. The tide turned when a friend challenged me to begin praying for this individual.

I prayed for this person's success in ministry. I prayed for them to have increased leadership skills to lead their teammates in the mission.

And it was really hard. In my heart, I wanted them to fail. Their failure would justify me and validate that my position was the correct one. But God used this process to soften my heart and put me on a path toward healing.

The world would encourage bitterness and payback. The Bible encourages us to turn the other cheek and to pray for people in our lives who frustrate us: "Love your enemies and pray for those who persecute you" (Matt. 5:44).

It may seem like a stretch to classify a bad coach as an enemy. It's probably an even greater stretch to associate the word *persecution* with mistreatment as an athlete. Regardless, the principle of praying for those you find difficult to like remains in effect.

So pray for your coach to know joy. Pray that you would find favor in your coach's eyes. Pray for his or her salvation. Pray for your coach's family and job. Pray for forgiveness for any sinful attitudes and actions related to your coach.

Let's go back to Madison Trout's story about the coach who stole her passion for her sport. Here's what she said in her open letter:

> When a passion dies, it is quite possibly the most heartbreaking thing ever. A desire you once had to play every second of the day is gone, it turns into dreading every practice and game. It turns into leaving every game with earphones in so other parents don't talk to you about it. It meant dreading school the next day due to everyone talking about the previous game.[3]

Trout allowed her coach to steal the keys to the joy of her sport. Don't make the same mistake. Fight for your joy by honoring your coach in every circumstance. In doing so, you will glorify your Father in heaven.

Questions for Individual Reflection or Team Study

Do not let this turn into a gossip session. Stay focused, and keep moving through the questions.

On a scale of 1–10, how hard is it for you to maintain a positive and godly attitude around your coach?

How could reflecting on the life, death, and resurrection of Jesus help you in your relationship with your coach?

What expectations do you have for your coach? Are any unrealistic? Have those expectations been communicated to him or her in a humble way?

How can you glorify God by the way you interact with your coach?

On a scale of 1–10, how often do you speak negatively about your coach behind his or her back?

What are a few reasons you are thankful for your coach?

What are some practical ways you can honor your coach as if honoring the Lord?

Take some time to pray for each other and your coaches.

Additional Questions for Coaches to Consider

If you surveyed your athletes anonymously and asked if they still found joy in playing their sport, what do you think they would say? What role, good or bad, do you think you play in their answer?

Do you have a filter or a set of safeguards you think through before communicating to your athletes? Do you think it would be helpful to have one? Why or why not?

Coaches are understandably frustrated a lot. What is your most common source of frustration or disappointment? What is your typical response to frustration and disappointment?

The word *coach* can be traced back to the idea of a stagecoach.[4] The purpose of a stagecoach is to get a person from one location to a new destination—quicker than that person could on his or her own. How do you do that today through sports? Where are you taking your athletes?

In your opinion, what is a God-honoring way to express frustration to your athletes?

If your athletes were a bank account, how could you put more credits than debits into your relational account with them?

12

On Mission

*I've been put here for a specific purpose: to be a witness
and to share my testimony as I go through it.*

Stephen Curry

Acts 17:26 says, "He made from one man every nation of mankind
to live on all the face of the earth, having determined allotted periods and the boundaries of their dwelling place."

God marked out our appointed times in history. He has a purpose for his people, and we see that in the time and location of their placement. It is no mistake that God has given you the abilities you possess. It is also no mistake that God has placed you where you are.

Why has he placed you there? To be a minister of reconciliation. Second Corinthians 5:18 says he "gave us the ministry of reconciliation." Us. You. Me. This is not a purpose or ministry given only to "professional" Christians but to all professing Christians. And professing Christians must know what to profess.

Where Do We Start?

I had just finished meeting with Warren when he stood up and exclaimed, "I am a dangerous man now!" Warren is a big guy—six feet two inches tall and three hundred pounds of muscle. He plays football—as if there were any other sport he could play at that size. As a defensive tackle, his job was to push other three-hundred-pound men out of the way and try to tackle whoever had the football in front of him. In his ideal world, he would crush the opposing player hard enough to dislodge the football. Yes, Warren was a very dangerous man.

But we were not talking about football. Warren had just been trained how to communicate what he believed about Jesus in four simple steps. It was the gospel: (1) God loves you; (2) your sin separates you from him; (3) Jesus paid the price for a restored relationship with you; (4) you have a decision to make. Upon learning this, something clicked in him. For the first time, he realized he had been equipped to fight battles, not on an earthly playing field but on an eternal one. Yes, Warren had just become really dangerous.

> It is no mistake that God has given you the abilities you possess. It is also no mistake that God has placed you where you are.

God gave you an athletic gift, and you are using it in a culture that worships sports heroes. Whether you like it or not, you are a difference maker. How are you stewarding that reality? As athletes, we bring glory to God when we speak well of him in public (Ps. 40:16). We should absolutely live a lifestyle on and off the field that honors God.

But we must also use words. When my son publicly tells his friends he has the best dad ever, it is a higher honor to me than when he merely tells me in the privacy of our house. God has given you a gift, a relationship with him, and a mouth to declare his goodness to a world that desperately needs it. We bring glory to him when we leverage this reality.

The purpose of this book is to help you learn how to glorify God in all the circumstances your sport provides. If you put even some of these ideas into practice, people will notice. And when they notice, they may become curious. So you'd better be prepared.

If somebody came up to you and said, "You seem different from other people—why is that?" how would you respond? First Peter 3:15 says we should always be prepared to answer a question like that. Here are two simple ways to be properly prepared to provide a reply:

1. Know God's Story

Simply put, know the gospel. Warren became dangerous because he learned how to communicate with someone else what he knew to be true. If you need a reminder of the gospel, turn back to chapter 1 and read under the heading "What Is the Gospel?"

2. Know Your Story

Aside from knowing the gospel, which is "the power of God" (Rom. 1:16), you need to learn your own story of how you came into a relationship with God. Your story helps explain why you are different.

If you claim to be a Christian and yet are unable to articulate either of these stories at some level, you are not very dangerous to the enemy. You are entering a war carrying a squirt gun and water balloons. To be an effective spiritual leader on your team, you need to learn how to articulate the gospel and how to put your story into words. Learn to do those two things and you will be dangerous. The appendix is dedicated to helping you tell your story. Trust me, if Jesus is your Savior and Lord, you have one worth telling.

What's Next?

You have been strategically placed on your team to impact its culture. To borrow a biblical metaphor, you are a light in a dark place. In Matthew 5:16, Jesus shares this with his followers: "In the same way, let your light shine before others, so that they may see your good works and give glory to your Father who is in heaven."

The ultimate goal of being a light on your team is not for your teammates to look up to you but for them to look *through* you and glorify God. How can you move in this direction? Let's talk strategy for a minute.

You will not change the current culture on your team by trying to change it. You will not alter the culture of your team by telling teammates to change the music in the weight room or imploring them to stop swearing in the locker room. Nor will you change the culture by telling teammates to stop partying or to stop putting harmful substances into their bodies. The you-need-to-stop-that strategy has proved to be ineffective. It makes you look judgmental by placing yourself above them, and it furthers the distance between them and God's best for their lives.

The best way to change the culture on your team is to create a new culture. Notice that there's a difference between trying to change the old or existing culture and creating an entirely new culture. The strategy shift is quite simple.

 You have been strategically placed on your team to impact its culture. To borrow a biblical metaphor, you are a light in a dark place.

Instead of serving as the morality police on your team, create new opportunities for them to think and act differently. Instead of walking into the darkness and saying, "Get out of here," shine a light on a better option. At some point, nearly everyone reaches a valley so low that they become starved for something that will satisfy. And many will be willing to try anything—even Jesus—at that point. So your role is to be ready to offer them something different when they are ready.

How do you go about creating a new culture? Here are a few ideas:

- Lead a prayer time before or after the game.
- Invite an injured friend over for dinner. Better yet, bring the dinner to your friend.
- Take every new teammate (the freshmen, if you're a student) out for coffee, and ask each one how the year is going and what you can do to help.
- Start a Bible study or find someone to start one for your team.
- Find a campus ministry, start attending their meetings, and invite teammates to go with you.

- Sign up for Ultimate Training Camp (UTC)[1] hosted by Athletes in Action, and bring some of your teammates with you. UTC helps athletes integrate faith and sport using Bible-based principles, Christian athlete community, and intense competition.

The 1989 classic movie *Field of Dreams* is about a farmer in Iowa who loves baseball. One day while out in his field, he hears a voice proclaim, "If you build it, he will come." The farmer eventually discerns that what he needs to build is a baseball field in the middle of his cornfield. People think he is crazy because nobody has ever done that before. It was not a regular part of the farming culture to turn a field of crops into a baseball field.

In reality, building a new culture doesn't guarantee that people will come. That's not your job anyway. God will always be the one who moves in people's hearts, spurring them to take action. Your responsibility is to faithfully work at providing a space for them to move to when God gives them that nudge.

A Few Thoughts on Bible Studies

There is a direct correlation between an individual's stagnant, immature faith and the lack of time he or she devotes to reading the Bible. A team Bible study could be one of the most effective ways to create a new culture on your team. But leading one of these groups can be scary and intimidating. I want to help demystify the team Bible study by giving you a few simple tracks to run down.

1. **Let people know about it.** Put the day, time, and location on the board in the locker room. Send out an email to the team. Make sure everyone knows it exists. Then individually invite your teammates. Asking each one personally creates a greater likelihood that people will come. It may feel a little awkward, especially if they decline your invitation, but get over it. Eternity is at stake.

2. **Be consistent.** Have your study on the same day, at the same time, and at the same location every week. If you are constantly changing times and places, your teammates will be confused. Confusion is a barrier for them showing up. Make it as easy as possible by keeping things the same.

3. **Show up and stay there.** If your Bible study is on Monday nights from 7:00 to 8:00 p.m., get there at 6:50 and stay there until 8:00, even if you are the only one who shows up.

4. **All you need is one other person.** If one teammate shows up, start the Bible study with that person. Don't sulk and make comments like, "Well, I guess we're the only ones," or "I wish more people would have come." Be excited for the person who came. God has a plan for that person—and for you.

5. **Read the Bible.** Don't overcomplicate a Bible study. Study the Bible. Work your way through one of the Gospels. Do a chapter each week. Read

the chapter out loud, and then talk through some simple questions. *What stands out to you in this chapter? What confuses you? What do we learn about God in this chapter? What questions do you have as we read through it? What do you think we can apply today from what we read?*

6. **Be okay with not having all the answers.** One of the big fears for anyone leading a Bible study is being asked a question and not knowing the answer. It is perfectly okay to not have all the answers. In fact, your teammates will appreciate your humility. When faced with a tough question, just say, "That's a great question, and honestly, I'm not sure how to answer it. Does anybody else want to take a stab at it?" If nobody advances the conversation, assure the individual that you will do some research and get back to him or her next week.

7. **Be okay with silence.** What if nobody talks? Sometimes, when there is silence, people feel uncomfortable or don't know what to say. Often, however, people just need time to think and process. Silence can be productive. After you ask a question, count to ten slowly in your head as you wait for a response. If nobody responds, ask if it would be helpful if you rephrased the question.

8. **Make one point.** One of the mistakes Bible study leaders make is trying to cram too much material

into one study. Think back to the last time you went to church. How much of the sermon do you remember? Probably very little. The Bible study is not your opportunity to knowledge-dump on your unsuspecting teammates. Don't overwhelm them. Find one major theme in the text and keep bringing them back to it.

9. **Be okay with rabbit trails.** Although your goal is to have one main takeaway, be okay with rabbit trails your teammates may want to go down. At the end of the day, the Bible study is for them. If they ask a question that is not relevant to what you are trying to do, feel the freedom to move in that direction. God may be up to something different than what you had planned.

10. **Pray.** Don't neglect this. It may be the most powerful thing that happens at the study. Bookend the Bible study with prayer. As you begin, ask God to help you all grow closer to him. As you finish up, ask for prayer requests from your teammates, and then pray for them according to their requests. The following week, ask them about the particular areas in their lives that you prayed about.

Athlete, God has a purpose for you where you are right now. You bring glory to him when you take faith steps to make an eternal impact.

Questions for Individual Reflection or Team Study

Who in your life has had the biggest impact on your spiritual journey? Why?

How would you communicate the essence of the gospel?

(This next question should take the bulk of the time.) What is your testimony (your personal journey of how you surrendered your life to Christ)?

What is the "spiritual climate" of your team? What is the team culture like?

What are some unique ways you could create a new spiritual culture on your team?

How receptive would your teammates be to you leading a team Bible study?

Additional Questions for Coaches to Consider

Does your team currently have a Bible study?

Have you ever encouraged one of your athletes to start a Bible study on the team? Why or why not?

Even if you are not in attendance (in fact, it's probably better that you're not), what are some ways you can help support the Bible study?

Do you think it's your responsibility to know the spiritual climate of your team? Why or why not?

Have you ever shared part of your faith journey (testimony) with an athlete or another coach? If not, why? If so, how did it go?

13

On Platform

*Sport has the power to change the world. It has the power to
inspire, it has the power to unite people in a way that little
else does. It speaks to youth in a language they understand.
Sport can create hope, where once there was only despair.*

Nelson Mandela

Christian athletes and fans generally love the concept of the athletic
platform. We love the idea that God has put certain individuals in
the spotlight and that those people can use their spotlight to talk
about Christ. We champion the reality that sports are a universal
language and a cultural megaphone that we can leverage for God's
glory.

To be honest, though, I'm tired of it. Not because I don't believe
in the power of a platform. After all, the mission statement of the
ministry I currently serve reads, "By serving, training, and sending
athletes as influencers into the world, we are building spiritual movements everywhere through the platform of sports so that everyone
knows someone who truly follows Jesus."[1] So it's part of my job to
care about platforms.

I also believe that having a platform is a biblical concept. Remember the story from Acts 14? The crowds were worshipping Paul and Barnabas because they had healed a man. The two men of God immediately deflected the praise lavished on them and sought to get the spotlight off themselves. But we need to finish the story because it doesn't end with them running from the crowd.

Everyone was cheering them on and watching their every move. They had a platform. The first thing they did was tell everyone to calm down because they were just men—not gods. This was not false humility but an earnest plea for the crowd to stop directing their praise at them. The last thing they wanted to do was steal any glory that belonged to the Lord. After putting a stop to the false worship going on, they started sharing the gospel with the crowd. Listen to how quickly they transitioned to sharing the good news:

> Men, why are you doing these things? We also are men, of like nature with you, and we bring you good news, that you should turn from these vain things to a living God, who made the heaven and the earth and the sea and all that is in them. (v. 15)

I've not grown tired of leveraging a platform for God's glory by sharing the gospel with a crowd that is hanging on every word. What I have grown tired of is how the idea of a platform has become reduced to a shout-out to God after a successful outcome.

The Christian athlete platform has come to mean this: people are watching, so make sure you give God credit. Somehow, we have assumed that lives can be transformed as a result of our verbally giving glory to God after a competition. It has become a box-checking exercise for "good" Christian athletes. It's a similar mindset to that of inviting our friends to church and assuming we've done our part once they get in the door, leaving the rest up to the pastor.

Your platform doesn't automatically make you an effective ambassador for Christ. It just means you have people's attention. If Christian athletes want to capitalize on the platform God has so graciously given to them, they need to pick their spots more strategically. A platform to spread God's love is an amazing gift, but it becomes most useful when it is leveraged with the right people in the right circumstances.

We need to clear up one more misconception about athletic platforms: that MVPs and stars are the only athletes who have a platform. They are not. If you are an athlete at any level of skill, you usually have a sphere of influence that surpasses the influence exerted by "regular people."

I believe an athlete's platform can especially influence younger teammates, the surrounding community, and social media followers. What follows is an encouragement to leverage your platform to these three groups, as well as practical tips on how to do it appropriately.

Engage Younger Teammates for God's Glory

To this day, I remember walking into the locker room as a freshman at Wake Forest University and having two significant encounters with seniors on the team in just the first week.

The first guy was Chris. He was the star of the track team. Fast, good-looking, extroverted. I will never forget entering that locker room shirtless, wearing black warm-ups, two-strapping my backpack, and my hat on backward. As I made my way to my locker, Chris looked at me and said affirmingly, "Smith, I like your style, man." I left practice that day with confidence. I was a skinny little runt, but this senior affirmed something he liked about me.

The second interaction came a few days later after a hard workout. I had developed blisters on the heels of my feet that began to bleed midway through practice. By the end of the afternoon, the backs of my new white training shoes were stained red.

Another senior, Ted, approached me as we were making our way toward the ice baths. Ted was not the most talented runner, but he worked his butt off. He was one of the best distance runners in the conference his junior and senior years. "Smith, you're gonna be one of the best to ever graduate from this school." He was way off. I ended up having a pretty awful running career. But more than fifteen years later, I can still recall how much I valued and appreciated that comment.

 Athletes bring glory to God when they go out of their way to speak life into their teammates.

What's the point of mentioning these interactions? Almost two decades have passed since that time, and I still remember them as if they were yesterday. Young athletes are impressionable. They are looking to follow someone's lead.

The Bible tells us that "death and life are in the power of the tongue" (Prov. 18:21). Our words carry a lot of weight. We have the opportunity through our words to be a fountain of life (10:11) and a tree of life (15:4) and to bring healing to others (12:18). Athletes bring glory to God when they go out of their way to speak life into their teammates. You have a platform with the younger people on your team. Take advantage of it.

Look for Ways to Serve in Your Community for God's Glory

As a competitive athlete, you have probably noticed that the crowd noise tends to get louder when you perform better. Unless you have parents who need to chill, the bulk of the crowd noise comes from members of the community who are cheering for you or the team you are representing. Those fans are comprised of teachers, parents, church members, alumni, children, and many others.

If you think they are excited when your team brings home a win, you should see how much more excited they'd get if you took time out of your schedule to talk to them.

Again, you do not need to be the star athlete on the team to do that. If you wear a jersey, you have a platform. One of the best ways you can leverage your platform as an athlete within your community is to share your testimony with local churches, youth groups, or elementary schools. (Check out the appendix to help you formulate your testimony.)

Rarely will these opportunities fall into your lap. They must be sought out. Make it a point in the next three months to contact a local church and say something like this: "My name is Brian, and I am on the cross-country team at Wake Forest University. I have been working on sharing my testimony, and I would love the opportunity to share it in front of the youth group at your church. Is this something you would be interested in and could help coordinate?"

If they say yes, bring a younger teammate with you.

Leverage Your Social Media Platform for God's Glory

As athletes, we can easily fall into the trap of thinking the content we fill our social media accounts with should be all about us. Christian athletes would be wise to leverage their social media accounts for the glory of God.

A business concept that's gained steam in the lives of individuals over the last few years is the idea of branding yourself. Simply put, this means making sure people see you in a certain light that benefits your long-term prospects and personal identity. Athletic departments all over the country are bringing in branding professionals to help athletes market themselves on and off the field. But for the Christian athlete, promoting yourself should always be a secondary concern. Don't be fooled by the hype. Whatever platform you currently have to influence others is a stewardship granted to you by God. He wants you to learn to use it for his purposes and not merely for your own.

I want to help you think about how to do that more effectively and to offer some tracks to run down that you may never have considered.

Get Better Simply by Avoiding Stupidity

Most advice for how athletes should behave on social media revolves around one theme: "Don't be a moron." It makes sense; people are watching.

Bret Bielema echoes the philosophy of many other coaches when he says he looks at the social media behavior of athletes he's deciding whether to recruit: "He's got to have a GPA that I can relate to, [a high] ACT or SAT score or a pre-ACT score, and the third box is for social media."[2]

Coaches pay attention to what their current and future athletes are doing on social media. But you already know that. NFL great JJ Watt once said:

> Read each tweet about 95 times before sending it. Look at every Instagram post about 95 times before you send it. A reputation takes years, and years, and years to build, and it takes one press of a button to ruin. So don't let that happen to you. Just be very smart about it.[3]

Coaches and players alike are learning that social media is a reflection of an athlete's character. Because this is true, most suggestions for how to use social media fall under the category of helping you not make a fool of yourself.

Like fire, social media has potential to do great harm if we are not careful with it. There is wisdom in exercising great caution when it comes to how it's handled. But it is also loaded with positive potential if we know how to use it correctly.

Don't Be Offensive—But Stay on Offense

Athletes have a platform, so it's good to know not merely how to avoid using it in ways that hurt you and others but also how to use it well. Followers of Christ need a higher standard for how to leverage our social media for the glory of God.

How many people are following you online? These people have chosen to pay attention to what you have to say on a daily basis. What are you feeding them?

Before we dive into the five practices you should be doing on your social media accounts, let me point out a couple things about social media:

1. Social media is different from any other media outlets. If you get interviewed after a game and talk about Jesus, the people watching, listening, and reading are, in a sense, forced to pay attention to you. It is why most people who are not Christians get annoyed when we talk about our faith. But in the world of social media, people *choose* to listen to you.

2. Whatever personal brand identity you are going for, if you are a follower of Christ, making him known should be a big part in that.

Since people are choosing to pay attention to what you have to say, here are five things you should be doing.

Share Edifying Content

You have an incredible opportunity to impact your audience by simply sharing good content with them. However, this assumes you know where to find it.

What do you regularly read or pay attention to that draws you closer to God? Hopefully, one of those streams you pull from is the Bible. If you haven't yet found an online source from which you consistently draw, here are a few recommendations: desiringgod.org, relevantmagazine.com, athletesinaction.org.

How you share something also matters. It's best to avoid only copying and pasting a link for your audience to click on. Give it your stamp of approval and make a comment about it. At the same time, understand that the majority of non-Christians consider Christians preachy and hypocritical, so you won't always get the response you'd like. That's okay. Be prepared for some backlash. Keep sowing seeds.

Here are a few creative ways to promote someone else's content in a way that is humble and thought-provoking:

- "This piece by _____ was super challenging to me. Check it out!"
- "I was so convicted after reading this. Take a look and let me know what you think."
- "Reading this really changed my perspective on _____. I think you will be challenged too!"

Encourage Your Followers to Follow Pastors, Ministry Leaders, and Sports Ministries

Introduce your followers to people and ministries who provide great Christian content to their followers. For example, here are the digital mission statements of a couple of the ministries I mentioned above:

- Desiring God exists to help people everywhere understand and embrace the truth that God is most glorified in us when we are most satisfied in Him.[4]
- Athletesinaction.org exists to help sports-minded people live and think biblically at the intersection of sports and Christianity.[5]

There are plenty of ministries and individuals out there whose mission is to provide faithful, relevant biblical content from which people can benefit. Is your mission to do something similar?

Probably not. And that's okay. Right now, you're focused on your sport. But God has gifted you with a talent that makes other people pay attention to you. Every once in a while, tell them to pay attention to someone else. Here are a couple of ways you might do that:

- Twitter: "If you're not following _____ already, I would highly encourage you to. He/she/they have helped me grow so much in my faith!"
- Facebook: "If you haven't liked the fan page of _____, do so now. With all the junk that comes across our newsfeeds, what he/she/they produce will be a refreshing change for you!"
- Instagram: "If you are not following _____, you need to start now! Check him/her/them out. You won't regret it!"

If those examples sound too much like a dad trying to be cool, come up with your own. The point remains: introduce "your" audience to spiritual influencers you have benefited from.

You are probably excellent at playing whatever sport God has gifted you to play. God has also gifted many pastors, writers, and ministry leaders at connecting with people about spiritual issues. Introduce your audience to people and ministries who specialize in delivering edifying digital content.

Repent Publicly and Privately

Having a platform also means that when you blow it big-time, everybody sees. But as a Christian athlete, you have the opportunity to show your followers that what separates Christians from everyone else is not moral perfection, but forgiveness. You can declare that God's forgiveness is not earned but given freely (Eph. 2:8–9). The Bible calls this *grace.*

If you end up cursing out an official, get on social media and apologize to your fans. To some extent at least, they view you as representing Jesus. If your sport is not televised, get on social media and tell your audience what happened, and then apologize. Don't make excuses. Apologize.

Sometimes we also need to repent privately about how we use social media. Most of us have been made aware of the dangers of making sport an idol in our lives. Countless articles, blogs, sermons, and chapel services have been created around the idea that we should not derive our identity from what we do on the playing field.

And yet … how many of us check our followers on a daily basis and gather a sense of satisfaction from the increasing numbers? How many of us feel a sense of pride as our fan base becomes more enamored with us? Conversely, how many of us feel inadequate in this area? How many of us wish we had thousands of people paying attention to what we have to say? If you find yourself in this category, I encourage you to repent to God for making social media an idol in your life.

Keep this in mind: What makes a Christian a Christian is that he or she is forgiven, not that he or she is perfect. When you screw up—and you will—know that your repentance is glorifying to God.

Be a Real Human

Post images and share about what you do on an everyday basis. Many people put athletes on a pedestal. Your sport gives you an elevated position in our culture. A 2013 study showed that athletes have more influence in our society than pastors.[6] People are listening to you because you are good at sports.

If you want to actually influence them, however, you need to show that you are like them. Your followers need to know that you are normal. When they see that you are just a regular person and then you offer a tweet like, "Check out this article from _____; it was super helpful for me in my walk with Christ," they are more likely to engage with you and the article.

Ask for Prayer

Whether you have three or three hundred thousand people who choose to pay attention to what you have to say, consider asking them to pray for you. As we've said, many fans put athletes on a pedestal. One way to actively push against that is to ask fans to pray for you. When you ask for prayer, you are humbling yourself and saying, "I need help," which is an expression of your need for God.

Encourage people to pray for you and for things that are important to you—a cultural event, things happening on campus or in the city where you play, a loved one in need, something happening at church, a Tweet or piece of social media, or a news story that caught your attention. Why not lead people to stop talking *about* you and instead encourage them to speak to God *alongside* you?

Eighty-two percent of Americans are on social media, and a handful of them are paying attention to you.[7] Keep learning how to be a good steward not only of the talent God has given you but also of the messages you communicate to the people who listen to what you have to say.

Should I Use My Platform in Pursuit of Justice?

Christians should be concerned about things that are not right in the world. With that in mind, should Christian athletes, who have a unique platform to speak to a listening world, speak up on issues of justice, or should they just stick to sports?

We can turn to one of my favorite stories in the Bible to help answer this. Esther is one of my heroes. I named my daughter after her Hebrew name, Hadassah. In the story, after the sitting queen decided not to show up in the king of Persia's presence, he dethroned her and chose Esther, a Jewish girl, to become his new queen. It's important to note that the king did not know Esther was Jewish.

Esther had an uncle named Mordecai. He heard that Haman, the right-hand man of the king, was putting a plan in motion to annihilate the Jewish population within Persia. Mordecai told Esther of the plan and urged her to stand in the gap for her people. He encouraged her to use her platform to seek the good of an oppressed people group. But Esther knew that if she came before the king without being summoned, he could have her executed. Esther faced great risk and sacrifice. Then Mordecai offered this plea to his niece:

> If you keep silent at this time, relief and deliverance will rise for the Jews from another place, but you and your father's house will perish. And who knows whether you have not come to the kingdom for such a time as this? (Est. 4:14)

Two things stand out to me in this verse. First, Mordecai was confident that God would bring about justice in this situation and that Esther had the ability to be God's chosen instrument. If she said no, Mordecai was confident God would use someone else. But secondly, he pointed out her platform: "Maybe, Esther, just maybe, you came into the kingdom for such a time as this."

 Why not lead people to stop talking *about* you and instead encourage them to speak to God *alongside* you?

Esther agreed, approached the king, found favor in his eyes, revealed Haman's treachery, and saved her people.

I want to introduce you to another hero of mine. Her name is Maya Moore. I first met Maya at Athletes in Action's Ultimate Training Camp in 2009. She was a star on the UConn women's basketball team. She led that team to a prolific 150-4 record that included four Final Four appearances and two national championships. Maya was just getting started. Since that time, here are a few of her noteworthy accomplishments:

- WNBA scoring title
- WNBA Rookie of the Year
- 4-time WNBA champion
- WNBA MVP
- WNBA Finals MVP
- 3-time WNBA All-Star Game MVP
- 2-time Olympic gold medalist

If she wasn't already the greatest female basketball player of her generation, she was well on her way. And then in 2019 she stepped away from the game. Why? To help a man named Jonathan Irons.

Jonathan was in prison, having already served more than twenty years of a fifty-year sentence for burglary and assault. Maya first met him in 2007 during a visit to the Jefferson City Correctional Center.[8] As she continued to build a relationship with Jonathan, she became convinced that he was innocent. This led her to walk away from the game of basketball for the next two years as she worked tirelessly on his case and helped fund efforts to see his sentence overturned.

On July 1, 2020, Jonathan Irons was released from prison. His sentence, with the help of Moore, had been overturned.

The shirt Maya wore as they embraced on that day reflects her core convictions and her journey over the course of those two years. It read "Micah 6:8," which says, "He has told you, O man, what is good; and what does the LORD require of you but to do justice, and to love kindness, and to walk humbly with your God?"

Now, I am not saying all Christian athletes need to follow Maya's lead and walk away from their sport. But if the spectrum of pursuing what is right through your athletic platform starts at nothing, on one extreme, and peaks at a Maya Moore–style sacrifice, on the other, you need to place yourself on it somewhere. Decide where, what, and how God is calling you to act—and then do something.

What does it look like for you to leverage your position of influence, as Esther and Maya did, for the good of those around you? At a minimum, this means a commitment to making sure all the members of your team are treated with the kindness, respect, and dignity they deserve. And when they're mistreated, either to their faces or behind their backs, you must stand up for them.

Why do any of this? Why should Christian athletes think deeply about what is wrong in the world around them? Because all of us are equal in God's eyes. All of us are uniquely created in his image. All of us "deserve to be treated with fairness and justice."[9] And when one of us isn't, it's the calling of God on our lives as his image bearers to stand in the gap for the oppressed.

Ultimately, we do it because Jesus did it for us. As God's Son, his "platform" was bigger than anything we could ever imagine. And yet he sacrificed everything—for us. Paul explained to the church at Philippi that our mindset should mirror Jesus':

Have this mind among yourselves, which is yours in Christ Jesus, who, though he was in the form of God, did not count equality with God a thing to be grasped, but emptied himself, by taking the form of a servant, being born in the likeness of men. And being found in human form, he humbled himself by becoming obedient to the point of death, even death on a cross. Therefore God has highly exalted him and bestowed on him the name that is above every name. (Phil. 2:5–9)

As you build your platform, recognize that at any point, God may ask you to step out of your comfort zone and help someone else. Who knows—maybe God gave you your athletic talent and put you where you are … for such a time as this.

Questions for Individual Reflection or Team Study

Which athlete do you look up to the most? Why?

What prevents you from investing in your younger teammates?

What would be some benefits of engaging with your younger teammates and speaking words of life into them?

What local churches, community groups, or youth groups could you share in front of? On a scale of 1–10, how comfortable would you be doing that?

If people looked through your social media accounts, how seriously would they think you take your faith?

What are some small shifts you can make to leverage your social media accounts for God's glory rather than your own?

When you think about your influence and the topic of justice, what comes to mind?

What, if any, action steps do you need to take to reflect Micah 6:8 and "do justice"?

Additional Questions for Coaches to Consider

People look up to your athletes simply because they are athletes. How could you help them use this for God's greater good?

What opportunities exist within your community that you could encourage your athletes to engage with?

How could you personally model utilizing the platform of sport for your athletes?

Jesus had a position of authority and chose to serve rather than be served. Do you think this is effective leadership? If so, what would this look like within your context?

14

On Retirement

One key to a meaningful transition is to retire
to something and not from something.

Bob Russell, *After 50 Years of Ministry*

Death. Taxes. Athletes retiring.

I know you don't want to read this chapter. The title alone reminds you of the truth that one day the sport you play will become the sport you used to play.

I don't know how it will end for you. It could be a career-ending injury. Maybe time will finally catch up with you and force you to call it quits, or maybe a diminishing skill level will prevent you from advancing to your next career goal. Maybe you're simply graduating from college with no future opportunities to continue playing. Whether you choose to hang up the cleats or it is somehow chosen for you, one day you will no longer be a competitive athlete. And that will probably be difficult to come to terms with.

Many of us struggle with the finality of our athletic career coming to a close. So we continue to chase after ways to keep it alive, often at lower levels of competition. Is there still the desire to make it to the pinnacle of success in our sport? There could be. But the more likely truth is that we don't want to stop competing—period.

The reality is that retirement is inevitable for every athlete. We all know the day is approaching, but it's hard to anticipate and process the feelings that come with that knowledge. Prim Siripipat, a former collegiate tennis player, once said:

> As tough as college was, no one warned me about an even greater challenge ahead: saying goodbye to the sport I love and making that transition into the "real world." The mental and emotional toll of this transition was a shock to my system.[1]

What Siripipat said can be attributed to anyone who has ever played competitive sports.

Dr. Henry Cloud points out in his book *How People Grow* that "One of the most important processes in life is grief. God has designed grief to help us get over things."[2] And make no mistake about it: moving on from your athletic career will be a grieving process. If done correctly, however, you will move through it in a way that honors God.

The purpose of this chapter is to help us glorify God through retirement. Part of that process involves practical advice on outward actions we would be wise to follow. But we first need to understand what is going on inside our hearts. Why is retirement so difficult for athletes?

A 2007 study reported:

The transition is often found to be difficult because of the sudden cessation of intense demands of elite athletic performance, compounded by the sudden loss of the athlete's intense devotion to professional athletic competition and its attendant rewards.[3]

What does all that mean? Understanding the process can help us transition from our sport to whatever God has in store for us next.

What Are We Leaving Behind?
The Hype (Rewards)

Boxing legend Sugar Ray Leonard famously said, "Nothing could satisfy me outside the ring. There is nothing in life that can compare to becoming a world champion, having your hand raised in that moment of glory, with thousands, millions of people cheering you on."[4]

While most of us will not be able to resonate with the feeling that comes from being a world champion and having millions of fans cheer us on, all athletes are in a unique position in culture to claim that at least some people have cheered for them. It's one of the rewards we desire most: the approval of others. You have no doubt experienced the hype leading up to a big competition and subsequently the hype of the contest itself. Even if you were not the center of attention, you were still part of the action. You played a role in the hype. And the hype is addictive.

Perhaps in your retirement, your new normal will not include crowds of people affirming you when you do your job well. The rewards for a job well done will look different. If you get an A on a test, maybe your family will pat you on the back. If you do well in your job, your affirmation may take the form of a bigger paycheck, but it definitely won't include everyone carrying you on their shoulders out of the office. The question that will—and should—haunt you in your next stage of life is this: For whom am I ultimately doing this?

Colossians 3:17 says, "Whatever you do, in word or deed, do everything in the name of the Lord Jesus, giving thanks to God the Father through him." Our motivation, whether in sports, school, work, or relationships should be to serve Jesus, not ourselves. Adjusting to life after the hype will be challenging, but it may be the very adjustment that helps you realign your motivation for the rest of your life.

The Competition (Elite Athletic Performance)

Athletes experience frequent highs and lows. We ride the roller coaster of emotions on such a regular basis that it almost becomes normal. Maybe day traders know these same extremes. Maybe parents. For some, the drama that comes with sports will not be missed. But for others, the addictive rush is hard to give up. Dr. Ed Uszynski writes:

> If you're an athlete, no rush compares to being physically challenged by another human who spends their days training to beat you—then either discovering you are equal to the challenge or having the areas you need to improve on exposed, thereby shaping the next days' workout.

The athletic psyche stalks challenge, seeks goals that push beyond barriers posed by normal life. Craving this bar-raising lifestyle can become almost addictive—and like other addictions, the grip happens without their knowledge or consent and is hard to get "fixed."

After decades of playing with elite-level players, kicking around at the local YMCA and retiring to backyard pick-up ball—while easily romanticized—is depressing, and every athlete who sees that future runs from it for as long as possible.[5]

The ups and downs of sports set a standard that could make the next stage of your life feel comparatively dull.

The Rhythms (Sudden Cessation of Intense Demands)

Dr. Uszynski goes on to explain the challenge:

There is a certain comfort that accompanies the boundaries to an athletic lifestyle. This can be replaced but it's not easy to find or come up with on one's own.

Retirement represents the death of an entire scheduling, relational, and subcultural lifestyle.[6]

At first, you will love the freedom that comes with being done with your sport. You get to sleep past 7:00 a.m. You get to eat freely. You get to choose when and where you want to work out—or if you want to work out at all. But you will eventually miss the structure you had, and the accountability you had within that structure. You will miss the rhythms of being a competitive athlete.

One might imagine that loosening the knot around the rigid structure would feel liberating, but often that is not the case. Athletes usually enjoy the free schedule at the beginning before ending up feeling lost without having to do things related to their sport—and for good reason. When your entire life is categorized by practices, workouts, nutrition guidelines, rest and recovery phases, and the orders of coaches and trainers, you are at high risk of becoming dependent on those structured systems in order to thrive.

 Your athletic career may be over, but God's calling on your life to be productive with your day still demands a response.

Matt Perman, author of *What's Best Next*, helps us understand why we thrive under structure. "Systems trump intentions. You can have great intentions, but if your life is set up in a way that is not in alignment with them, you will be frustrated. The structure of your life will win out every time."[7]

Did you catch that last sentence? Structure matters. You will be tempted to binge-watch Netflix and sleep in every day until it's time to eat lunch. Don't. Your athletic career may be over, but God's calling on your life to be productive with your day still demands a response.

Ephesians 5:15–16 says, "Look carefully then how you walk, not as unwise but as wise, making the best use of the time, because the days are evil." The intense demands and structure of your sport may be gone, but don't use that as an excuse to become lazy. Glorify God by moving your disciplined structure of living into a new passion or hobby that serves others and makes much of Jesus.

The Sense of Purpose (Intense Devotion)

Our purpose will always flow from our identity. How we view ourselves determines what we do—and being an athlete is usually a huge part of a person's self-concept. Even in this book, I have addressed you as an athlete. The implications of this can be damaging when retirement comes. The following thoughts from Dr. Monica Frank should resonate:

> It is critical to recognize that the athlete's self-identity is typically inseparable from their role as an athlete. Often for many years the major focus in their life is on developing as an athlete and succeeding in their chosen sport. When the sports career ends, it leaves a major hole in the athlete's life. Whether the career ended as planned or suddenly, the athlete experiences a significant loss that can be as devastating as losing a loved one. The end of the career doesn't mean just not engaging in the sport anymore. It also changes the athlete's role: he or she is no longer an "athlete."[8]

If God graciously allows you to experience his love through sports and gives you the opportunity to glorify him through your athletic career, that's awesome. But whether you identify as an athlete, father, mother, friend, accountant, janitor, husband, or wife, your ultimate purpose never changes. Christian, you were placed on this earth to glorify God through loving him and serving others. Your purpose does not change—only the vehicle that drives you there.

Your permanent purpose is to glorify God by loving him and loving others. You used to spend much of your time and energy attempting to do this through your sport. Now that sports are in the rearview mirror, you need a new vehicle to drive you toward this purpose.

What's Next?

Preparation will always make transitions easier. Dr. Henry Cloud and Dr. John Townsend point out: "We must have something good in hand to be able to let go of something bad. It is a little like being a trapeze artist: You can only let go of one trapeze if another is in view."[9]

The easiest way to move on from sports is to replace the role that sports played with something else. Here is the reality. When your sport ends, you will have space in your life that did not exist before. You will have time. And that time needs to be stewarded well.

The remainder of this chapter could be filled with jab after jab about ideas and strategies to cope with the transition. But I want to give you a right hook. I want to give you one big, God-glorifying way to transition out of your athletic career wisely.

Ready? I want to challenge you to get involved in the mission of God. What would it look like for you to shift your focus from the earthly scoreboard that sports rely on to God's eternal scoreboard, which is characterized by lives transformed by the finished work of Jesus?

 The church is the primary way God has chosen to reach the world with his love.

Hopefully, this book has encouraged you to leverage your sport in a way that glorifies God while you play it. But when your sport is over, the call to glorify God with your life doesn't retire with it. What opportunities exist for you to partner with God in the next stage of your life? Where can you combine your passions and gifts to impact others? If you can't think of any, let me suggest one for you to consider: the church.

I know some of you may cringe at that statement. Many young people have had a bad experience with a church or have avoided getting involved in one for other reasons. Let me say this as gently as I can: it's time to re-engage. The church is God's main vehicle for influencing the world.

Francis Chan doesn't mince words: "We can't claim to follow Jesus if we neglect the church He created, the church He died for, the church He entrusted His mission to.... The church is God's strategy for reaching our world."[10]

Now that you're retired, you no longer have the excuse of competing and traveling on the weekends. You can no longer leverage your coach's early Sunday morning workouts as a way out. To some degree, every athlete's church involvement is negatively affected by the demands of his or her sport.

The church is the primary way God has chosen to reach the world with his love. If that's not motivation enough to get involved, there is another factor that may capture your attention. Some of the same things you came to love and enjoy through sports can be experienced at an even deeper level through the local church. The dangling carrot of contentment you so desperately sought through sports can be obtained through the local church. Let me explain by working back through some of the benefits of sports that you will be leaving behind.

The Hype (Rewards)

Can anything compare with achieving an athletic goal and having teammates, coaches, and fans affirm the accomplishment? Absolutely. If you have ever played a role in seeing God transform someone's life, you know firsthand that no athletic performance will ever compare. Transformation trumps trophies.

What would it look like for you to use your God-given gifts to help make a kingdom-sized dent for the glory of God?

Involving yourself in the mission of God in this next stage of your life is not only glorifying to God; it also meets your desire to be a part of something greater than yourself.

As God's primary strategy to reach a lost world, the church stands on the front lines. By linking arms with the church, you put yourself in prime position to see God transform the lives of men and

women in your community, country, and the world. If you are looking to set high goals and are willing to rely on God to come through
for you, you will not find many better options than getting involved
with the local church.

The Competition (Elite Athletic Performance)

We love to think of athletic talent as a gift from God. It certainly
is, but when the Bible speaks of gifts from the Lord, it is talking not
about genetic dispositions but spiritual additions. For too long, you
have been led to believe that the gifts God has given you are primarily your athletic abilities. It is time to learn that God has given you
a different gift—one that is to be stewarded not for your own glory
or the benefit of screaming fans but for the good of God's people.

> Having gifts that differ according to the grace given
> to us, let us use them: if prophecy, in proportion to
> our faith; if service, in our serving; the one who
> teaches, in his teaching; the one who exhorts, in his
> exhortation; the one who contributes, in generos-
> ity; the one who leads, with zeal; the one who does
> acts of mercy, with cheerfulness. (Rom. 12:6–8)

Each of us who has been reconciled to God through belief in
the gospel has been given one or more spiritual gifts by the Holy
Spirit for the benefit of his people. What would it look like for you
to use your God-given gifts to help make a kingdom-sized dent for
the glory of God?

One of the best settings to learn and use what spiritual gifts you have is within the community of other Christ-followers committed to growing together and sharpening one another.

The Rhythms (Sudden Cessation of Intense Demands)

Your life and schedule used to be centered around the demands of your sport. Now it's time to find a better center. Check out what 1 Timothy 4:8 says: "While bodily training is of some value, godliness is of value in every way, as it holds promise for the present life and also for the life to come."

Your structured way of living around sports produced some value. What if your new structure involved significant involvement and blocks of time given to the mission of God? This verse clearly shows that a pursuit of godliness has both present value and eternal value. A commitment to pursuing others with the gospel, especially within the context of a church, provides a rhythmic structure to help you in this area.

The Sense of Purpose (Intense Devotion)

For the retired Christian athlete, the calling on his or her life will continue to flow from what is often called the Great Commission. In these verses, Jesus instructs *all* his followers to "Go therefore and make disciples of all nations, baptizing them in the name of the Father and of the Son and of the Holy Spirit, teaching them to observe all that I have commanded you. And behold, I am with you always, to the end of the age" (Matt. 28:19–20).

John Piper boldly lays out our three options in response to this: "There are three possibilities with the Great Commission. You can go. You can send. Or you can be disobedient. Ignoring the cause is not a Christian option."[11]

You can help fulfill the Great Commission through the avenue of sports. The purpose of the church is to love God and love our neighbors while working to see the Great Commission fulfilled. The church's mission focuses on this goal. Against the backdrop of eternity, knowing God and doing his will—including sharing the good news with others—easily trumps any other goal you could strive for.

If you are feeling lost and confused as you struggle to make sense of your retirement, why not join the greatest mission in the history of the world? The church is waiting for you.

J. Campbell White said it well:

> Most men are not satisfied with the permanent output of their lives. Nothing can wholly satisfy the life of Christ within his followers except the adoption of Christ's purpose toward the world he came to redeem. Fame, pleasure, and riches are but husks and ashes in contrast with the boundless and abiding joy of working with God for the fulfillment of his eternal plans. The men who are putting everything into Christ's undertaking are getting out of life its sweetest and most priceless rewards.[12]

Athlete—I mean, Christian—mourn the loss of your sport. But mourn quickly. Lift your head and direct your time, talents, and energy into God's plan to see lives transformed for his glory, and be part of the greatest mission this world has ever known.

Questions for Individual Reflection or Team Study

What comes to your mind when you think of retirement?

The author writes: "The ups and downs of sports set a standard that could make the next stage of your life feel comparatively dull." What are some of the unique highs and lows that come with playing sports?

What will you miss most when you can no longer compete at your current level?

What has been your experience with the church?

Are you part of a local church right now? Why or why not?

Is it hard for you to see the comparison between sport and the mission of the church? Why or why not?

What do you think of John Piper's quote? "There are three possibilities with the Great Commission. You can go. You can send. Or you can be disobedient. Ignoring the cause is not a Christian option."

Additional Questions for Coaches to Consider

What is your coaching philosophy about having practice on Sunday mornings?

Do you prioritize church attendance for yourself and your athletes?

When you hear the word *community*, who comes to mind? Who are the key people in your life that you can be honest with and be challenged by?

Do you think it's your responsibility to create space for your athletes to attend church if they want to go? Why or why not?

Do you think it's your responsibility to help your athletes be prepared for life after sport? Why or why not?

Conclusion

We don't obey Jesus to get something from Jesus. We obey because he gave us himself. We get him. He is the treasure.

Derwin L. Gray, *Limitless Life*

In the fall of 2007, I did something stupid: I signed up to compete in an Ironman. After watching the race take place in Madison, Wisconsin, I thought, *I could do that.* So I signed up the next day.

After a year of training, I toed the line on September 11, 2008, at Ironman Wisconsin, with my sights set on qualifying for the World Championship in Kona. After a 2.4-mile swim, a 112-mile bike ride, and 26.2-mile run, I came up about six places shy of my goal. (It didn't help that my right knee decided to stop working with about 10 miles to go on the run.) The competition took me ten hours and twenty-five minutes to complete.

A day later, I sat down in front of a computer and typed up my summary of the race, detailing every bit of it I could recall. Today, although I remember a few distinct moments from that day, most of it is a blur. But if I hadn't written that recap, many of the amazing memories from the competition would have been lost.

Maybe you're feeling that way right now. You have read through this entire book. Hopefully, there were some "aha" moments and practical tips that will help you leverage your sport for God's glory. But perhaps you have forgotten the majority of it. It was a lot of information. So a recap could help you retain some key points.

Introduction

- We need to learn how and execute on making our sport serve us in a way that draws us closer to God.
- When we use our sport to get more of God, we are aligning ourselves with the way God intended his good gifts, like sports, to work.
- Ecclesiastes 3:11 says that God has put eternity in our hearts. The implication is simple: we cannot be satisfied by earthly things.

Chapter 1: On Glory and God

- What God desires most is his glory. As John Piper says, "God has many other goals in what he does. But none of them is more ultimate than this."[1]
- *Glory* simply means "weight."
- Giving God glory means thinking and acting in a way that pleases him and draws attention to who he is.
- God is not indifferent to anything that takes place within his universe, which includes how you play and think about your sport.

- The gospel shows us that God is pleased with us not because of anything we do or did but because of what Jesus has already done for us.
- We must view God through the lens he wants to be viewed through—as our Father.

Chapter 2: On Motivation

- We often wrongly believe that Philippians 4:13 means we can achieve any outcome in our sport because of Christ.
- In its proper context, Philippians 4:13 means that we can have contentment regardless of the outcome because of Christ.
- A focal point is something you can quickly concentrate on that realigns your focus on your ultimate motivation in your sport: glorifying God.

Chapter 3: On Pressure

- If motivation is the unseen reason for doing something, pressure is the unseen reality causing unwanted friction for your motivation.
- Mantras like "nobody cares, work harder" may sound catchy, but they contribute to poor mental health and stand in opposition to God's call for us to steward our hearts and minds.
- Struggles with pressure and mental health are hardly new categories for a God who has seen it all.

- Identifying the inner pressures we are facing and having a game plan for training our minds are the first steps toward achieving a healthy mental state (inner peace).

Chapter 4: On Winning

- Celebrating good things that happen is not evidence of a lack of humility; it is part of how God designed us to react.
- Winning is great, and we should desire to pursue it, but there is a good reason why it does not satisfy you at a soul level. It was never supposed to.
- Don't relegate giving your best to game-day performances. Don't be habitually lazy in practice, in the weight room, and with your eating and sleeping habits, and then give it 100 percent during competition and claim, "All glory to God!"
- Go ahead and pray for the win.
- Accept praise humbly and graciously.

Chapter 5: On Losing

- It's all right to be frustrated when you lose. You're human. Don't fake positive emotion to appear godly.
- When a Christian athlete loses and still makes much of Jesus, non-Christians notice and often want to know more from that athlete. Anyone can make much of Jesus after a win.

- Our obedience should be birthed out of a desire to please our heavenly Father, not out of a misguided belief that our goodness can be exchanged for an earthly blessing like athletic success. God is not a genie.

Chapter 6: On Injuries

- Be honest with God about how you are feeling; he can handle it.
- God may be preparing you for something in the future through your current circumstance.
- God may want you to deal with something in the present, and your injury is the pause on which you need to focus.
- You may be injured because God wants to use you to reach someone else.

Chapter 7: On Practice

- For Christian athletes, practice should primarily be about others, not themselves.
- Your motivation in practice should be to engage in it as if you were doing it for the Lord.
- Relationships will always have more lasting value and joy than the trophies you earn.
- God has designed our bodies in such a way that when we exercise, we experience increased happiness (endorphins, etc.).

Chapter 8: On Teammates

- Despite unfortunate circumstances, Jonathan chose to act as a faithful friend instead of complaining.
- Great teammates seek to put others above themselves, especially at times when it's hardest to do so.
- Great teammates do not lurk behind the scenes looking for opportunities to capitalize on the misfortune of others.
- Your most significant impact as an athlete may be on the teammates you rub shoulders with every day.

Chapter 9: On Riding the Bench

- Honoring the Lord through our sport should not be contingent on our ability to actually see the playing field.
- You glorify God from the bench when you're open to the possibility that God may have you on the team for purposes other than winning a championship.
- Trust that God knows what he is doing in your life. This lack of playing time is part of his plan for you.

Chapter 10: On Gray Areas

- God stared into the face of chaos and created order. What does that look like in sports? Simply put, we follow the rules of the game.

- When we choose to operate with integrity in every way possible, we image our Creator.
- Doing the right thing doesn't mean you'll come out on top of the scoreboard.
- Athletes who take a hard line on gray areas are susceptible to becoming prideful or at least being seen as prideful. Be aware of what's going on in your heart and how others might see you. If following all the rules—obeying the letter of the law—creates pride, it's sin. Attitude counts too.

Chapter 11: On Coaches

- It's our job as God's lights in this dark world to submit, smile, and display the life and love of Jesus when in harsh and unfair situations.
- You can avoid a lot of disappointment if you release any unrealistic expectations you may have placed on your coach.
- When you show the desire to be a continual learner, you honor your coach as the teacher—and bring glory to God.
- Christian athletes are called to stand out from the crowd, to look different. Resist the urge to gossip about your coach.

Chapter 12: On Mission

- The best way to change the culture on your team is to create a new culture.

- To be an effective spiritual leader on your team, you need to learn how to articulate the gospel and how to put your story into words.
- A team Bible study can be one of the most effective ways you can create a new culture on your team.

Chapter 13: On Platform

- Your platform does not automatically make you an effective ambassador for Christ. It just means you have people's attention.
- If you have veteran status on the team—and if you don't now, you will someday—you have a platform to speak words of life into younger athletes on the team.
- Opportunities to leverage your platform will rarely fall into your lap. You must seek them out.
- Use your social media to strategically engage your followers. Remember, they chose to follow you, so don't be afraid to be bold.

Chapter 14: On Retirement

- Moving on from your athletic career often involves a grieving process. It can be hard. That's a natural reaction to losing something and should be expected.
- The ups and downs of sports can set a standard of excitement that makes the next stage of your life feel comparatively dull.

- Many of the same things you enjoyed in your sport can be found and experienced through involvement in the local church.

Last Word

There is one last thing I want to remind you of before the close of this book. Do you remember our discussion about Paul and Barnabas in Acts 14 and how their story provides a model for the modern-day Christian athlete to follow? Let's briefly review what happened.

- They did something amazing (healed a man).
- The crowds around them went crazy, worshipping the two men as if they were gods.
- They responded in humility by saying they were not gods but just normal guys like everyone else.
- But now they had a platform. People started paying attention to what they were saying. They knew the gospel well and used this opportunity to share with the crowd about the one true God.

What else could God ask of these two? They were intentional, skillful, humble, and opportunistic. Surely, God would bless their efforts, right? Let's see.

Even with these words they scarcely restrained the people from offering sacrifice to them. But Jews

> came from Antioch and Iconium, and having per-
> suaded the crowds, they stoned Paul and dragged
> him out of the city, supposing that he was dead.
> (vv. 18–19)

Are you kidding me?

They did everything God asked of them, yet somehow the crowds turned on them, and Paul got stoned to the point that he appeared to be dead.

Well, he wasn't dead. And when he finally came to, what do you think he did? What would *you* do in that situation?

> But when the disciples gathered about him, he
> rose up and entered the city, and on the next day
> he went on with Barnabas to Derbe. When they
> had preached the gospel to that city and had made
> many disciples, they returned to Lystra and to
> Iconium and to Antioch, strengthening the souls of
> the disciples, encouraging them to continue in the
> faith, and saying that through many tribulations
> we must enter the kingdom of God. (vv. 20–22)

Let this story and others like it in the Bible serve to teach you a fundamental truth: Obedience to God does not mean things will play out as we would like. My hope is that you put into practice as many things in this book as possible, but please, please, do not think that just because you begin to give glory to God through your sport, he is now obligated to grant you athletic success in return. He might. But he might not.

> Obedience to God does not mean things will play out as we would like.

Your obedience and willingness to glorify him should not come with strings attached. Struggles and hardships will come. They always do. Be ready for them.

My prayer for you is that your response to adversity will be similar to Paul's and that you will persevere when things get tough. My prayer is that when you fall, you will get back up, surrounded by a community to help you tend to your wounds and get back into the game, trusting that God will sustain you as you seek to give him the glory due his name through your sport and through your life.

At the beginning of the book, I challenged you with this question: "God, what do you even want from me as an athlete?" Now I hope you have the answer. He wants your whole heart.

Appendix

How to Craft Your Sports Testimony

Follow the chart below, and work through the corresponding template to craft your testimony.[1] If you email it to me at Brian.Smith@ athletesinaction.org, I will look it over and give you some feedback!

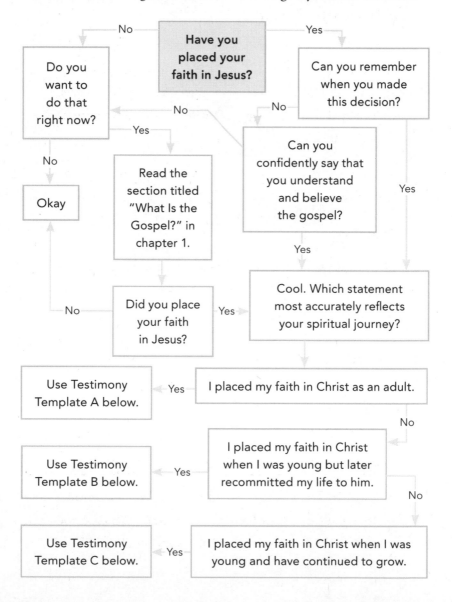

Christian Athlete Testimony Template A

Life before Christ

1. What things were you looking for in life—and maybe specifically in your sport—that were not bringing you the satisfaction you thought they would? (For a lot of athletes, it's things like approval from others, identity as an athlete, or performance-based acceptance.)

2. Give one example of how you tried to chase after this need unsuccessfully.

Transition

"But no matter how much I _____, it never satisfied me the way I expected it to."

   Or

"But no matter what _____, I was never fully content."

   Or

"Even though I achieved _____, I still felt empty inside."

How You Surrendered Your Life to Christ

1. Describe what happened that caused you to consider inviting Jesus into your life for the first time. Who did you talk to? What did they say? What clicked inside you for it all to make sense?

2. State how you trusted Christ. Briefly include the gospel message. (Sharing the gospel could include but not be limited to saying something like this: "I finally put my faith in Jesus. I realized I was separated from God because of my sin and that Jesus died and rose from the dead to make a way for me to be in relationship with God.")

Transition

"I don't have all the answers, but I am confident that
_____."

   Or

"I am still a work in progress. But since I trusted Christ, I have noticed _____."

Life after That Decision

1. Describe what your walk with God has looked like since you made the decision to follow him (in three to five sentences).

2. A couple ways to end: You could recite your favorite verse and briefly state why it's your favorite. You could, in your own words, admit you are still on a journey but that you are trusting God to grow you according to his perfect timing. Or you might, in your own words, restate how you still struggle with the things in life you were chasing from the very first question but how you have confidence that God is with you and helping you see that a relationship with him is better than those things.

Christian Athlete Testimony Template B

Life before Christ

1. Describe what happened that caused you to consider inviting Jesus into your life for the first time. Who did you talk to? What did they say? What clicked inside you for it all to make sense? Include the gospel message. (Sharing the gospel could include but not be limited to saying something like this: "At a young age I realized I was separated from God because of my sin and that Jesus died and rose from the dead to make a way for me to be in relationship with God.")

2. What caused you to fall away? What lies were you believing? Or, what things were you looking for in life—and maybe specifically in your sport—that were not bringing you the satisfaction you thought they would? (For a lot of athletes, it's things like approval from others, identity as an athlete, or performance-based acceptance.)

Transition

"Even though I know that Christ never left me, I felt like I left him because _____."

    Or

"I am confident that God's love for me never changed, but my love for him seemed to change because _____ _____."

Or

"I wouldn't say I fell away from God, but something just did not seem right in my heart because _____."

How You Surrendered Your Life To Christ

What happened that caused you to recommit your life to Jesus? Who did you talk to? What did they say? What clicked inside you for it all to make sense?

Transition

"I am still a work in progress, but since I recommitted my life to Christ, I have noticed _____."

Life after That Decision

1. Describe what your walk with God has looked like since you made the decision to follow him (in three to five sentences).

2. A couple ways to end: You could recite your favorite verse and briefly state why it's your favorite. You could, in your own words, admit you are still on a journey but that you are trusting God to grow you according to his perfect timing. Or you might, in your own words, restate how you still struggle with the things in life you were chasing from the very first question but how you have confidence that God is with you and helping you see that a relationship with him is better than those things.

Christian Athlete Testimony Template C

How You Surrendered Your Life to Christ

1. Describe what happened that caused you to consider inviting Jesus into your life for the first time. Who did you talk to? What did they say? What clicked inside you for it all to make sense? Include the gospel message. (Sharing the gospel could include but not be limited to saying something like this: "At a young age I realized I was separated from God because of my sin and that Jesus died and rose from the dead to make a way for me to be in relationship with God.")

2. In three to five sentences, state how God has helped you grow in your relationship with him through a specific experience you had as an athlete or maybe a specific relationship with someone else in your life.

Transition

"I don't have all the answers, but I am confident that _____."

    Or

"I am still a work in progress, but since I trusted Christ, I have noticed _____."

    Or

"As I follow Jesus, he continues to transform me. One of the areas I am growing in is _____."

Life after That Decision

1. Describe what your walk with God has looked like since you made the decision to follow him (in three to five sentences).

2. A couple ways to end: You could recite your favorite verse and briefly state why it's your favorite. Or you might, in your own words, admit you are still on a journey but you are trusting God to grow you according to his perfect timing. You could also, in your own words, share what you are currently struggling with but that you have confidence that God is with you in the middle of the struggle.

Acknowledgments

To all the financial and prayer supporters of our ministry with Athletes in Action: We promised you when we joined the staff that we would do more than sit in coffee shops all day. (Confession: I spent a lot of time in coffee shops working on this. Hopefully, the end will justify the means.) Thank you for your partnership in the gospel with Linsey and me. This book is a result of your investment in us.

To Linsey: You are—and always will be—my best friend and the love of my life. This book didn't happen without your affirmation of me as a man, a writer, and a minister of the gospel. You gave me confidence and freedom (and time away from the house projects) to see this book to the finish line.

Notes

Chapter 1: On Glory and God

1. John Piper, *Desiring God: Meditations of a Christian Hedonist* (Colorado Springs: WaterBrook, 2011), 42–43.

2. This list of "glory" verses was adapted from John Piper, "Biblical Texts to Show God's Zeal for His Own Glory," desiringGod, November 24, 2007, www .desiringgod.org/articles/biblical-texts-to-show-gods-zeal-for-his-own-glory.

3. Timothy Keller (@timkellernyc). 2014. "What is the glory of God?" Twitter, August 13, 2014, 5:00 p.m., https://twitter.com/timkellernyc/status /499691880540823552.

4. John Piper, "What Is God's Glory?," desiringGod, July 6, 2009, www .desiringgod.org/interviews/what-is-gods-glory.

5. J. I. Packer, *Knowing God* (Downers Grove, IL: InterVarsity, 1973), 200.

6. C. S. Lewis, *Reflections on the Psalms* (New York: Harcourt, Brace and World, 1958), 97.

7. Ed Uszynski, "Does God Care Who Wins?," Athletes in Action, accessed July 9, 2021, https://athletesinaction.org/articles/does-god-care-who-wins.

8. Richard J. Mouw, *Abraham Kuyper: A Short and Personal Introduction* (Grand Rapids, MI: Eerdmans, 2011), 4.

Chapter 2: On Motivation

1. C. S. Lewis, *The Weight of Glory* (San Francisco: HarperCollins, 2001), 26.

2. Kevin Black, "The Truth That Helped Helen Maroulis Transcend Gold: How Identity in Christ Changes Our Approach to Sports," Athletes in Action,

accessed July 9, 2021, https://athletesinaction.org/articles/the-truth-that-
helped-helen-maroulis-transcend-gold.

3. Paul David Tripp, *New Morning Mercies: A Daily Gospel Devotional* (Wheaton,
IL: Crossway, 2014), June 22.

4. Wes Neal, *Handbook on Athletic Perfection* (Grand Island, NE: Cross Training
Publishing, 2003), 132.

5. This concept is taught every year at Athletes in Action's Ultimate Training
Camps. It's commonly referred to as "Down time is His time."

Chapter 3: On Pressure

1. Kate Fagan, "Split Image," ESPN, May 7, 2015, www.espn.com/espn/feature
/story/_/id/12833146/instagram-account-university-pennsylvania-runner
-showed-only-part-story.

2. Joe Padilla and Matthew Stanford, *Thrive: Living Resilient and Renewed*
(Waco, TX: Mental Health Grace Alliance, 2015), 6, https://static1.square
space.com/static/5a9d8fb47c9327e01e4b3451/t/5e724b8e4d66ee1209e
6eb56/1584548763843/THRIVE+free.pdf.

3. Rachel Arnold and David Fletcher, "A research synthesis and taxonomic
classification of the organizational stressors encountered by sport performers,"
Journal of Sport and Exercise Psychology 34, no. 3 (June 2012): 397–429, doi:
10.1123/jsep.34.3.39.

4. Jocko Willink and Leif Babin, *Extreme Ownership: How U.S. Navy SEALs
Lead and Win* (New York: St. Martin's Press, 2015).

5. Nancy Armour, "Why college football player's death should terrify parents,"
USA Today, June 26, 2018, www.usatoday.com/story/sports/columnist/nancy
-armour/2018/06/26/washington-state-qb-committed-suicide-but-football-killed
-him/734604002.

6. Andrew Wolanin et al, "Prevalence of clinically elevated depressive symptoms
in college athletes and differences by gender and sport," *British Journal of
Medicine* 50, no. 3 (February 2016): 167–71, doi: 10.1136/bjsports-2015
-095756.

7. Matthew S. Stanford, *Grace for the Afflicted: A Clinical and Biblical Perspective
on Mental Illness* (Downers Grove, IL: IVP Books, 2017), 90–94.

8. Stanford, *Grace for the Afflicted*, 106–110.

9. Stanford, *Grace for the Afflicted*, 164–166.

10. Stanford, *Grace for the Afflicted*, 140–142.

11. Stanford, *Grace for the Afflicted*, 142–143

12. Stanford, *Grace for the Afflicted*, 162–164.

13. Russ Rauch and Ginger Gilmore Childress, "Raising the Tide of Mental Wellness," NACDA 53, no. 4 (December 2018): 34, www.visionpursue
.com/wp-content/uploads/2019/01/Raising-the-Tide-of-Mental-Wellness
-NACDA.pdf.

14. Rauch and Gilmore Childress, "Raising the Tide."

15. Craig Groeschel, *Hope in the Dark: Believing God is Good When Life is Not* (Grand Rapids, MI: Zondervan, 2018), 64.

16. Groeschel, *Hope in the Dark*.

Chapter 4: On Winning

1. C. S. Lewis, *Reflections on the Psalms* (New York: Harcourt, Brace and World, 1958), 95.

2. "Tom Brady on winning: There's 'got to be more than this,'" *60 Minutes*, aired January 30, 2019, YouTube video, www.youtube.com/watch?v=-TA4
_fVkv3c.

3. Herbert McCabe, *God, Christ, and Us* (London: Continuum, 2005), 105, used by permission of Bloomsbury Publishing.

4. Sam Crabtree, *Practicing Affirmation: God-Centered Praise of Those Who Are Not God* (Wheaton, IL: Crossway, 2011), 127–128.

Chapter 5: On Losing

1. Stephen Altrogge, *Gameday for the Glory of God: A Guide for Athletes, Fans and Wannabes* (Wheaton, IL: Crossway, 2008), 79–81.

2. Altrogge, *Gameday*, 83.

3. Don Pearson and Paul Santhouse, *YOUthwork: Let God Use Your Influence* (Chicago: Moody Publishers, 2009), 33–34.

4. Attributed to Dr. Seuss, AZ Quotes, accessed July 9, 2021, www.azquotes
.com/quote/922897.

Chapter 6: On Injuries

1. Henry Cloud, *Changes That Heal: Four Practical Steps to a Happier, Healthier You* (Grand Rapids, MI: Zondervan, 1992), 25.

2. Kaitlin Miller, "Don't Resent God's Training Ground," desiringGod, January 31, 2017, www.desiringgod.org/articles/don-t-resent-god-s-training-ground.

3. Matt Chandler, "Of Danger and Ditches," Village Church Resources, March 15, 2008, www.tvcresources.net/resource-library/sermons/of-danger-and-ditches.

4. Craig Groeschel, *Hope in the Dark: Believing God Is Good When Life Is Not* (Grand Rapids, MI: Zondervan, 2018), 64–65.

Chapter 7: On Practice

1. Leo Widrich, "What Happens to Our Brains When We Exercise and How It Makes Us Happier," Buffer (blog), August 23, 2012, https://blog.bufferapp.com/why-exercising-makes-us-happier.

2. M. K. McGovern, "The Effects of Exercise on the Brain," Serendip, Spring 2005, https://serendipstudio.org/bb/neuro/neuro05/web2/mmcgovern.html#:~:text=MK%20McGovern,pain%2C%20both%20physical%20and%20mental.

Chapter 10: On Gray Areas

1. Jeff Bradley, "Brian Davis Taught Us Integrity, Honesty," ESPN, April 19, 2011, www.espn.com/golf/columns/story?id=6375777&columnist=bradley_jeff.

2. Bradley, "Brian Davis."

3. Cambridge Dictionary, s.v. "gray area," 2021, https://dictionary.cambridge.org/us/dictionary/english/gray-area.

4. Ed Uszynski, "Your Call?," Athletes in Action, January 25, 2016, accessed March 15, 2018, https://athletesinaction.org/your-call#.WYzlRcbMyt8.

Chapter 11: On Coaches

1. Madison Trout, "The Coach That Killed My Passion: An open letter to the coach that made me hate a sport I once loved," Odyssey, August 15, 2016, www.theodysseyonline.com/to-the-coach-that-killed-my-passion.

2. Matthew C. Mitchell, *Resisting Gossip: Winning the War of the Wagging Tongue* (Fort Washington, PA: CLC Publications, 2013), 23.

3. Trout, "The Coach That Killed My Passion."

4. Dictionary.com, s.v. "coach," 2021, www.dictionary.com/browse/coach.

Chapter 12: On Mission

1. For more information on UTC and to sign up, visit: https://athletesinaction .org/utc.

Chapter 13: On Platform

1. "About," Athletes in Action, https://athletesinaction.org/about/ mission-vision-values.

2. "Bad Behavior on Social Media Can Cost Student Athletes," CBS News, August 11, 2014, www.cbsnews.com/news/bad-behavior-on-social-media-can -cost-student-athletes.

3. Doug Samuels, "JJ Watt Shares Some Social Media Advice for High School Athletes," Football Scoop, July 17, 2015, http://footballscoop.com/news /jj-watt-has-some-social-media-advice-for-high-school-athletes.

4. John Piper, "The Story of Ian & Larissa," desiringGod, May 8, 2012, www .desiringgod.org/articles/the-story-of-ian-larissa.

5. Athletes in Action (@AIAusa). 2016. "To help sports-minded people think and live biblically at the intersection of sport and Christianity." Twitter, February 18, 2016, https://twitter.com/aiausa?lang=en#:~:text=Athletes%20 In%20Action%20(%40AIAusa)%20%7C%20Twitter.

6. "Athletes Influence Greater than Faith Leaders," Barna, April 10, 2013, www.barna.com/research/athletes-influence-greater-than-faith-leaders.

7. H. Tankosvska, "Percentage of US population who currently use any social media from 2008 to 2021," Statista, April 14, 2021, www.statista .com/statistics/273476/percentage-of-us-population-with-a-social-network -profile.

8. Minyvonne Burke, "WNBA star Maya Moore to sit out season and Olympics as she advocates for inmate's release," NBC News, January 23, 2020, www .nbcnews.com/news/sports/wnba-star-maya-moore-sit-out-season-olympics -she-advocates-n1121441.

9. "Justice," Bible Project, https://bibleproject.com/explore/justice.

Chapter 14: On Retirement

1. Prim Siripipat, "Moving on from Sports: A College Athlete's Greatest Challenge," ESPN, April 11, 2016, www.espn.com/espnw/voices/article /15182997/moving-sports-college-athlete-greatest-challenge.

2. Henry Cloud and John Townsend, *How People Grow: What the Bible Reveals about Personal Growth* (Grand Rapids, MI: Zondervan, 2001), 135.

3. Emma Vickers, "Life after Sport: Depression in the Retired Athlete," BelievePerform, accessed July 7, 2021, http://believeperform.com/wellbeing /life-after-sport-depression-in-retired-athletes.

4. Peter Crutchley, "Why Do So Many Athletes Struggle to Cope with Retirement?," BBC Sport, December 18, 2012, http://beta.bbc.com/sport /0/20646102.

5. Ed Uszynski, "The 5 Reasons Athletes Can't Retire," Athletes in Action, accessed July 9, 2021, https://athletesinaction.org/underreview/the-5-reasons -athletes-cant-retire#.WYzo58bMyt9.

6. Uszynski, "The 5 Reasons."

7. Matt Perman, *What's Best Next: How the Gospel Transforms the Way You Get Things Done* (Grand Rapids, MI: Zondervan, 2014), 193.

8. Monica A. Frank, "Issues When Ending a Sports Career," Excel at Life, 2002, www.excelatlife.com/articles/ending_career.htm.

9. Cloud and Townsend, *How People Grow*, 136.

10. Francis Chan, *Multiply: Disciples Making Disciples* (Colorado Springs: David C Cook, 2012), 52.

11. John Piper, *Brothers, We Are Not Professionals: A Plea to Pastors for Radical Ministry* (Nashville: B&H Publishing Group, 2013), 219.

12. J. Campbell White, quoted in John Piper, "There Is No Greater Satisfaction: God-Centered Motivation for World Missions," desiringGod, October 1, 1990, www.desiringgod.org/articles/there-is-no-greater-satisfaction.

Conclusion

1. John Piper, *Desiring God: Meditations of a Christian Hedonist* (Colorado Springs: WaterBrook, 2011), 42.

Appendix: How to Craft Your Sports Testimony

1. "How to Share Your Testimony" is copyrighted by Navigators Church Ministries of the Navigators and has been adapted with permission for an athletic audience.